GROWIN

M000196560

BY

Robert Atkinson

;

By the same author

QUEST FOR THE GRIFFON

.

ED

To Patsy

for much help and encouragement

CONTENTS

ILLUSTRATIONS

FIGURES

PLATES

FOREWORD

THIS short book reviews the ways and means of modern commercial apple growing, with the interests of an intending planter on a limited scale, with limited resources, particularly in mind. Current practice and developing trends are fully covered, and special emphasis is given to the problems of planning so long term an investment as an apple orchard. The approach is practical, though comprehensive and detailed instruction in matters like pruning or the techniques of grafting has had to be summarized in the space available. Excellent manuals dealing with such subjects already exist – notably some publications of the Ministry of Agriculture – and the more essential ones are listed in a bibliographical note at the end of the book.

Courses in fruit growing are run by some Agricultural Colleges and County Farm Institutes, and some commercial growers take pupils. Age and ambition usually decide whether or not a new grower undergoes any initial training. It is well to remember that the National Agricultural Advisory Service is instructional as well as advisory; to the untrained planter the County Horticultural Officer offers the best means both of contact with the fruit growing industry and of help in practical difficulties.

Chapter One

THE INDUSTRY

A PIECE of orchard near the house is an immemorial part of the landscape of English farming, though nowadays old farm orchards often provide little more than shade and shelter for stock. The grass below is more valuable than the apples above, and when the big ungainly trees do bear a crop it is virtually unsaleable. It is just as well. The days when such rough farm fruit went to market, jumbled into wicker-work sieves and baskets, have all but passed; the woven baskets and the horses and carts have gone, replaced by loads of cheap wooden boxes piled on to lorries and driven away from factory-like packhouses; and the appearance of the fruit carried off to market has improved and improved. English apples in the shops may not always seem very wonderful but they are probably a better sample now than they have ever been.

Fruit-growing for market has been a recognizable commercial activity for three centuries but its development into a specialized field industry in its own right is much more recent. A good deal of apple-growing, chiefly of cooking apples, does remain an aside to general farming, and market gardening often continues in traditional association with fruit-growing. Change, as usual, has been in the direction of specialization: no sooner had the fruit farm developed into an entity than the number of sorts of fruit grown began to be curtailed and then the number of different varieties of any one fruit. Only a small proportion of top fruit orchards are still under-planted with soft fruit. Apples are and will no doubt continue to be the mainstay of English fruit growing; so, with increasing specialization, farms growing nothing but apples are now common enough. Everything is bought in, no stock is kept, nothing is sold off except apples. New holdings, particularly those planted by new-

9

comers to the industry, are commonly of this degree. All the eggs are in one basket but this is often the modern way.

This sort of specialization began to develop towards the end of the nineteenth century, even as commercial apple-planting developed overseas. Overseas planting in fact, directed at the English market, has been a considerable spur to home growers, and the home and overseas industries have grown up together. The dry sunny climates of overseas orchards produced brilliantly red fruit and overseas growers were at once forced into strict grading and packing techniques, because only best fruit was worth sending on such huge journeys. In England the first grading machines used by progressive growers were imported from America.

Fortunately for the English grower, quality of imported fruit has never equalled home-grown. Bulk shipments from overseas in the time between the wars showed the state of affairs: hard, bright red, tasteless apples from abroad, as alike as peas in a pod, against the often rough-looking ill-presented English fruit of incomparably better taste. And in the overseas orchards, garish sun above and irrigation channels in the dust, against the slow, English, autumn days of sun and dew drench, as mellow as an old brick wall; wax doll apples against the awkward natives. Home growers have never suffered competition on grounds of quality alone, except possibly in the out-of-date case of Newtown Pippins from North America, only on appearance; and they are mending their ways as fast as the markets and the foreigners force them to. In fairness it must be remembered that the whole of the commercial home crop, which is bound to include a proportion of low-grade fruit, has to be marketed at home, whereas of course overseas growers export only their best grades and have to get rid of the rest in their own countries. From 1928 until the war the National Mark much improved matters; the grades were statutory but their adoption or not by individual growers was voluntary. Quality suffered a setback during the war, with imports stopped and with ministerial emphasis on maximum home production, plus guaranteed prices.

'Home-grown rubbish' is still unfortunately plentiful enough both in local shops and national markets, but the amount decreases every year, and the ill-reputation of English fruit is gradually being repaired. Nowadays there is nothing to choose between the best home-grown and the best imported apples in matters of grading, packing and appearance; the colour of imported fruit is often brighter, but the quality of home-grown is as far ahead as ever.

Specialization in the modern apple growing industry is seen at its limit in a plantation of Cox's Orange Pippins. The trees are compact bushes on a single short stem, each exactly like the next, and so precisely set out that, as the viewpoint changes, they fall into fascinating geometrical patterns as row after row opens and shuts. The trees grow from a greensward as close as a lawn; gang mowers spin up and down the rows, spouting green showers of grass, as though the place was some municipal park. Monstrous machines trundle slowly past, blanketed in their own swirling spray, leaving the trees dripping with a selection of poisons beyond the dreams of the British Pharmacopoeia. At blossom time hundreds of smudge-pots smother the district in black smuts; at harvest time, inside the barbed wire and netting fence, an army of pickers pick apples, still with their own unaided hands. Such plantations have their beauty, but it is less careless than that of bygone trees. The tractors draw gently away low platform trailers laden with the precious tons of pippins, into a factory of pallets and fork-lift trucks, gas chambers, gravity conveyors, and double bank graders, all in an industrial clatter. At the far end are the same old greengrocers' shops, and peering housewives.

In spite of the existence of hundred-acre and even larger fruit farms, mechanized to the hilt, apples are still primarily a small grower's crop. Probably some 30,000 men make at any rate part of their living by growing apples on some 170,000 acres. This does not include cider apples, the acreage of which has been dropping for many years and whose future appears annually more gloomy. The average holding is surprisingly small, between four and five acres. Holdings of between one and five acres (more than 21,000) make up 56 per cent of the total number and 28 per cent of the apple acreage; five to ten acre holdings (5,000) make 13 per cent of the total and 20 per cent of the acreage; ten to twenty acres (2,000), between 5 and 6 per cent and 16 per cent; and over twenty acres (1,200) 3 and 33 per cent. There are only about 300 farms with more than fifty acres of apples and they make up 16 per cent of the apple acreage; but there are still over 8,000 holdings of less than one acre, making 22 per cent of the total number but only 2½ per cent of the acreage.

Tradition, as much as rainfall, elevation and suitable land, has set the distribution of orchards. Apples are essentially an English crop of the midland and southern counties; acreage in northern England, Scotland and Wales is negligible and Northern Ireland manages only cookers. The chief districts are well defined: the south-eastern counties (Kent still has nearly a third of the total apple acreage); the bleak flat lands of East Anglia, with Essex particularly noted for new plantations of dessert apples; the hills and dales of the West Midlands (Hereford, Worcester, Gloucester, Warwick); and the drier districts of the south-west (parts of Somerset and Devon), the last two areas containing a good proportion of cider orchards. Successful dessert apple orchards lie strictly within a minimum average day temperature isotherm of 68°F for July and August, and of 64°F for September; their rainfall does not exceed 35 in. annually or their elevation 500 ft. above sea level.

Some 180,000 tons of dessert apples and 325,000 tons of cookers were produced in the United Kingdom in 1953, and a further 118,000 tons were imported. The division between cooking and dessert apple varieties is largely native; elsewhere apples are just apples, and the same varieties are used indifferently both raw and for cooking. In England only three different sorts of apples can claim the status of national varieties, one cooker, Bramley's

Seedling, and two dessert apples, Worcester Pearmain and Cox's Orange Pippin. These same varieties can be made a commercial success on five acres or on five hundred; the wide range of scales that can succeed is like pig or poultry keeping but not, for instance, like dairying or arable farming.

The Ministry of Agriculture has carried out Fruit Tree Censuses from time to time since 1925. The two post-war censuses of 1944 and 1951, with other compulsory returns made by growers, show that the enormous preponderance of post-war planting has been of dessert apples, with Cox far and away the most favourite variety. Before the war Worcester was the recognized national dessert apple, now it is undoubtedly Cox — the easiest of all apples to sell and one of the most difficult to grow. There are now reckoned to be slightly over 10 million dessert apple trees planted in England, and just over half of them are Cox. Nearly 3 million of the Cox trees are post-war plantings, mostly not yet in full bearing. Cooking-apple trees number between 4 and 5 million. The world population of apples is estimated to be some 400 million trees.

Expansion of the apple acreage in England has been going on since 1920 and has considerably quickened since the war. Of late years the expansion has been of dessert apples only, and cooking apples have shown a net loss in acreage. Before long there will be double the immediate post-war tonnage of Cox alone to market. On top of home expansion there have been heavy post-war plantings on the Continent, chiefly of Cox, Jonathan and Golden Delicious, and primarily directed at the English market. Some people assume that expansion will go on until the bottom drops out of the market. Dollar difficulties have provided fortuitous protection from the North American crop since the war, but this is now ending. The only imported apples which do not compete with home-grown are from the Southern Hemisphere; the Granny Smiths and the Sturmer Pippins of Australasia begin to arrive as the stored home crop finishes in the spring, and come to an end, or should do, when the new home crop begins again in August. Overseas growers are often assisted by their governments; the home grower is not. Unlike general agriculture fruit-growing is in no way supported by any system of guaranteed markets and prices or by subsidies; fruit, vegetables and flowers go to market and fetch what the buyer, if any, offers, while the increase in costs of labour, fuel, fertilizers and so on is the same for growers as for subsidized farmers. The promise of the 1947 Agriculture Act that horticulture would be given the same stability as other branches of agriculture has never been implemented, and it is difficult to see how it ever could be without close governmental control of crop acreage and marketing, not to mention pests and diseases and seasonal hazards. Revised tariffs now give some protection to many home-grown vegetables and fruits, but not to apples. Apple imports are at present regulated on a quota basis, free of import duty; half a million pounds' worth was the permitted ration for the period July 1–December 31, 1954. Imports from Commonwealth countries (except Canada) are on Open General Licence. At home, a government grant has been instituted recently to pay up to half the cost of grubbing derelict orchards.

So far, since the war, the more efficient apple-growers have managed to offset much of their increased costs by better management, giving bigger yields per acre of better quality fruit; this, with better grading and packing, and more use of storage to extend the marketing season, has of course involved them in very heavy capital expense. The remarkable freedom of the post-war period (so far) from bad May frosts has also been a tremendous help; an apparent three-year cycle of spring frosts began in 1935 but ended in 1944. Increased costs are only too well known – none more vociferous about them than farmers – but apple prices have nowhere near kept in step. At Christmas time in 1938, English Cox were making up to 44s a bushel at Covent Garden. Admittedly 1938 was a year of spring frost and very light crops, but 44s a bushel for best Cox is rather better than the average mid-winter prices of the last few years. Apple-growers by their own unaided efforts have done well to survive and even to flourish in post-war conditions, but it is unlikely that sustained high yields per acre, which is the heart of the matter, can be increased much more. Costs of growing go on increasing, but apple prices are much more likely to drop than to rise.

Even so, many growers, and particularly the larger and more efficient, who have built up their own packing and marketing organizations, prefer to be left to find their own salvation. This was well shown by the fate of the proposed Apple and Pear Marketing Board in the spring of 1953. This scheme was sponsored by the National Farmers' Union and among other things the Board was hoping to promote apple sales as well as preventing low-grade apples from reaching the fresh fruit markets. It was also supposed to be going to have some say in the control of imports. Any grower with more than one acre or fifty trees was entitled to register as a producer and then to vote for or against the scheme. About 32,000 registration papers were sent out but only between 16,000 and 17,000 were returned, and just under 11,000 growers actually voted. A two-thirds majority both of growers and of the acreage they represented was required to bring the Board to life. Three-quarters of the growers voted in favour of the scheme, but the orchards they represented – 65,000 acres – just failed to make a two-thirds majority over the 40,000 acres of those who voted against. By and large, it was the smaller growers who were worried about the future and who were ready to accept some direction and to pay a small levy in exchange for more orderly marketing; larger growers preferred to be left alone. Since then there has been some talk of re-introducing the National Mark, but it has had very little support. There is now little chance of any new marketing scheme coming forward for several years, much to many growers' regret. Marketing continues as before, with most of the apple crop sold by commission salesmen in the major fruit and vegetable markets of London (Covent Garden and

Spitalfields), Glasgow, Newcastle, Leeds, Manchester, Birmingham, Bristol and Southampton. Growers' auctions are also held in some fruit-growing areas.

Fruit-growers are particularly well served by research stations and the link between grower and scientist is closer than in other branches of agriculture. East Malling, near Maidstone, and Long Ashton, near Bristol, are the two senior fruit research stations. Both deal with all aspects of fruit-growing, though East Malling is particularly noted for many years' work on rootstocks and Long Ashton for important discoveries in fruit-tree nutrition. East Malling started as a chip from Wye Agricultural College in 1913 and now covers over 300 acres and employs a scientific staff of some 130 research workers. Nearly 2,000 growers are members of the East Malling Association; their subscriptions help to support the station and in return they receive the annual report and can attend the several Open Days held each year, when aspects of current research are demonstrated. Members can also buy surplus nursery material.

Long Ashton started life as the National Fruit and Cider Institute in 1903, and dealt only in cider-making until 1912, when experiments in general fruit-growing began. Long Ashton's interest in cider continues, with the new technique of growing cider apples as bush trees in a mown sward – like 'shop' apples – instead of as a happy-go-lucky mixture of old unsprayed standards and grazing stock. Anyone interested in the possibilities of new planting of cider apples should go to Long Ashton; they have a membership scheme like East Malling's. Both stations are engaged in fruit-tree breeding, though no new apples likely to be universally planted have yet emerged. Such topical problems as mineral deficiencies in apple trees, the management, constitution and effects of orchard cover crops, and the embarrassing new subject of virus diseases, are being investigated by both stations, and both sustain the perennial contest between sprays and pests. Other horticultural research stations deal with fruit-growing, notably the John Innes Horticultural

Institution, whose new cherries are a great success and one or two of whose new apples seem likely to find a place in commercial orchards. Many experiments in the storage of apples have been made in the Ditton Laboratory at East Malling, run by the Food Investigation Organization of the Department of Scientific and Industrial Research. The most urgent of present research problems are probably the breeding of a new good quality August dessert apple and the finding of ways of growing and storing Cox to lengthen its marketing season.

The link between growers and research staffs is perhaps not so close as it used to be before the introduction of the National Agricultural Advisory Service. Chatty AGM's and cricket matches go on as before, but the routine advisory work is now ably handled by the NAAS. This service is organized on a county basis and each county has a Horticultural Officer. The counties are grouped into several provinces, each of which, in the fruit growing areas, has a Provincial Fruit Specialist. Growers' queries are supposed to go through the sieve of Horticultural Officer and Fruit Specialist before reaching the research stations, though this does not always happen and research workers are still found in growers' orchards, to their mutual benefit. Private fruit consultants find there is still a niche left for them, like private doctors and dentists, and old hands as well as new-comers often find their services well worth the fee.

The National Fruit Trials are another great aid to growers. The Trials were established at Wisley, Surrey, in 1921, jointly by the Royal Horticultural Society and the Ministry of Agriculture, to test new varieties of all hardy fruits. New varieties admitted for trial are matched against accepted standard varieties chosen for each season. Naturally the great majority of new seedlings are found wanting and this negative sifting is an invaluable service, saving growers much time and disappointment. The Trials are now moving to a new site in Kent, as, unfortunately, the Wisley orchards are at the bottom of a bad frost hole and spring frosts have rather vitiated the value of the trials.

B

The Horticultural Branch of the National Farmers' Union looks after the interests of fruit-growers, and its Fruit Committee is always sparring with the Ministry of Agriculture, spurred on by a never-ending string of resolutions from the county branches. The industry is big enough to support a number of ancillaries, such as spray chemical and machinery manufacturers, horticultural sundriesmen, boxmakers and of course wholesale nurserymen. The bigger firms run whole advisory services of their own, and their travellers are usually full of news and information, and carry gossip from one orchard to the next. The big chemical firms usually have their own trial orchards. Fruit growers share two trade papers with other horticulturists, *The Grower* and *The Commercial Grower*, and fruit news is also printed in the general farming papers, *Farmer's Weekly* and *Farmer and Stockbreeder*.

Fruit-growing was once rather a family affair, the lore passed from father to son, but since it became an industry all sorts of people with no previous connection with the land have joined in. Many ex-officers started fruit-growing after 1918, many more after 1945. As in pig and poultry keeping and market gardening, there have been plenty of failures but never any lack of new entries. No branch of agriculture now shows the brightness of immediate post-war prospects, though apple-growing still looks as well as any. Tree-fruit growing is very inflexible; a grower cannot suddenly switch to another crop or type of husbandry, but a new planter is at least not saddled with an orchard of outdated varieties.

Not the least of the usefulness of state research stations has been their taking up, testing and dissemination of the best commercial practice. Many of the problems of growing apples can be considered well enough solved, and much of the speculation has been transferred to the question of whether there is room for still more new planting. Consumption of fresh fruit in 1952 was still well below the pre-war rate and apple sales are actually decreasing, though not of the best varieties, where demand probably still exceeds supply. There has been no revival of advertising campaigns like the 'Eat More Fruit' of pre-war days. The matter of advertising is being discussed now, but the difficulty of financing it appears to be insuperable at present. It will no doubt have to come, and the same problem already exists more sharply in America; I read in the *American Fruit Grower* that 'it should not be too difficult a job to sell more people on using apples regularly' so it is to be hoped that the same will apply in Britain.

At present an accepted commercial crop of dessert apples is an annual average of five tons an acre, or about 250 bushels. Profits vary enormously; in well managed orchards of good dessert varieties, bearing heavily, the margin of sales over current expenses is of the order of £100 an acre. Certainly the best growers are making a living now, but what any intending planter wants is an answer to the question 'If I plant so many acres of apples and spend so many pounds, shall I eventually get an economic return?' It is an unanswerable question and different people give different guesses, because all depends on the state of affairs in ten or twenty years' time. Freer trade? Foreign dumping? Tariff walls, war, peace, slump, prosperity?

England's future, so everyone says, is in quality goods, and England can grow the best dessert apples in the world. Now that growing them has become an industry in itself, and a vested interest to many other industries, any early limit to its expansion is hardly to be expected. Wholesale nurserymen's sales are still (1954) far higher than replacement of over-aged trees can account for and, at the other end, there are signs that eventually an export trade in Cox may develop. I think there are still good prospects in dessert apple growing and I don't think the small man need be swamped; but success will strictly depend on the ability to produce heavy, clean crops of the very few right varieties, well coloured, the right size, carefully graded and packed.

Chapter Two

THE TREES

THE apple pip planted by Mr Richard Cox, retired brewer, in his garden at Colnbrook, Bucks, about the year 1830, grew and bore fruit and was named by him, Cox's Orange Pippin. Without knowing it, Mr Cox founded an industry because every Cox tree, past, present or future, ultimately derives from buds of the original tree at Colnbrook. Apples do not come even approximately true from seed – with rare exceptions – and so have to be propagated vegetatively. They will not strike from cuttings, so budding and grafting have to be used; varieties thus propagated appear to be immortal, however limited the life-span of each tree. All cultivated apple trees (except original seedlings) are therefore deliberate creations, a chosen scion married to a chosen rootstock. The rootstocks used for apples are themselves apples, though selected not for the fruit they might bear but for the influences, such as size of tree and precocity of cropping, that they exert on varieties worked on to them. Rootstocks are also propagated vegetatively, although a few seedlings – called 'free' or 'crab' stocks and grown from cider apple or wild crab pips – are still sometimes used, as in the old days; they give unpredictable results but usually make big trees.

Over two thousand different named varieties of apples are known in England alone, yet those successful in commerce number twenty at most and only three can be called national varieties. A variety comes to the fore for two main reasons, either for its exceptional quality — as in Cox among apples and Doyenné du Comice among pears, Royal Sovereign among strawberries, Leveller among gooseberries – or for its sterling reliability – as in Worcester and Bramley apples, Conference pears, Victoria plums. Reliability means the production year after year of heavy crops of apples of which at least 80 per cent comes into top grade, which will travel and store and not show bruises, which look attractive and are sweet as well as juicy, and which sell freely in the markets; it is a searching combination of qualities. The reason why so many varieties remain 'garden apples' is simply that either they are not reliable enough or if of exceptional quality then not exceptional enough or combined with damning characteristics, like poor appearance. So often choice garden varieties give of their best only in a favourable year, whereas Cox with all its temperament yet achieves at least a recognizable degree of the famous Cox flavour under all sorts and conditions of season, soil and management. It is encouraging that in our shoddy age of mass production anything so difficult as a Cox's Orange Pippin should have become a national favourite on grounds of quality alone; the market was waiting for it long before growers had learnt to produce it.

Here then are the dessert apples that have either emerged from garden to commercial orchard, or have come straight from the plant breeders, divided, according to season, into Early, Second Early, Mid-season, Winter and Early Spring varieties. Cooking apples follow them.

Early Dessert Apples.—Pretty little Beauty of Bath opens the season early in August, when apples come again: a poor thing, yet the earliest dessert apple grown in any quantity. The flat, round fruit is very summery and attractive in its dappled scarlet and green, and a red tinge spreads into the flesh; it starts fresh-tasting but rather too acid and soon goes mealy. The tree is a strong grower, slow to crop, with stiff horizontal branches that seldom break away from the trunk even when the angle of the crotch is narrow. Bath is well known for dropping its fruit before it is ripe, but reacts well to pre-harvest hormone spraying (see p 100). It is not worth planting on grounds of quality, yet there is nothing else in its season. No one would now think of planting Gladstone, small, mealy and ready to burst like a baked potato, or Devonshire Quarrenden, hard and scabby. Of newer varieties, Laxton's Early Crimson is too small and too poor; Laxton's Advance is sweet and of good flavour – in fact bird pecking is a problem with the variety – but it is a poor cropper and of indifferent appearance; Maidstone Favourite is much like Bath and is no improvement on it, except that it crops better. Melba is nearer the mark, a Canadian apple, colourful, sweet and juicy, but condemned by being really too soft to travel, by inclining to biennial bearing and by undue liability to scab. A brighter coloured sport from it, Red Melba, does not ripen until late August, is firmer and less liable to scab; it would have a better chance if it ripened three weeks earlier.

Second Early Dessert Apples.—The end of August sees the first pickings of Worcester Pearmain, and it was in the hope of preventing the rush of unripe green Worcesters on to the market that East Malling bred and introduced Tydeman's Early Worcester, a cross between Worcester and the Canadian McIntosh. A good many growers are giving this tough-skinned, densely red apple a trial; it ripens up to ten days earlier than Worcester proper and is of better flavour, though nothing very wonderful. The tree grows strongly and fills itself with bare wood unless carefully pruned. A far better quality variety at the beginning of the Worcester season is Laxton's Epicure, extraordinarily sweet, but unfortunately full of defects; its greenish-yellow, red flushed appearance is not bright enough, its fruit is too long in the stalk and sets in clusters like cherries that require drastic thinning, and its season of good flavour is very short. Even so, its good quality, heavy cropping and healthy growth may keep it in commerce in a small way, particularly where there is a local holiday market. Epicure makes a stalwart, rather spare tree that crops heavily from the start. Of the same season Miller's Seedling – smooth, nearly white with a faint flush when ripe, and fresh-tasting – is attractively easy to grow, being practically scab proof. But it is a confirmed biennial bearer and although at the end of the war, when nursery stocks were so low, a galaxy of authority – the Ministry of Agriculture, National Farmers' Union, Royal Horticultural

Society and Horticultural Trades Association – included it with Cox, Worcester and Superb for quantity production, it is little planted now. Some growers in early districts can get it coloured and saleable early in August, and then it is more valuable.

The sight of an orchard of Worcesters ready for harvest, the trees settled into mounds with the weight of brilliant red fruit, is enough to explain its popularity. The apples are the right size and the right colour; they pack and travel admirably; they submit to months of gas storage, so that nowadays Worcesters are in the shops from late August until the New Year, and they have even been held until May. The trees blossom unfailingly – making the variety a splendid pollinator – and crop enormously; some growers manage five and six hundred bushels an acre for seasons together. Yet no one pretends that Worcester is a first-quality apple; many of the complaints against it are due to its being marketed when the base colour is still green, but even when fully ripe, abundantly sweet and juicy, it is one of those tough-skinned dense fruits that can be chewed and chewed and never grow less; yet it happily surpasses imported apples on grounds of quality. Worcester is a wonderful apple which will take a lot of superseding, but there is enough of it already planted, and it has a promising challenger.

In Fortune there is at last a September apple that when well grown and fully ripe can be spoken of in the same breath as Cox. Its season is almost exactly that of Worcester, though it keeps a little longer in natural store, and in some seasons ripens patchily and prematurely so that the trees can be picked over at the end of August. In the markets well-presented samples already make a premium over Worcester. Fortune is far the best of Messrs Laxton's many introductions and has the same parentage as Epicure (Wealthy × Cox); many growers back it for a great future and it is the first variety of the season that can be wholeheartedly recommended to a new planter. Fortune appears to be blessed with an excellent constitution; its tough dark green leaves are slow to show any mineral deficiency, and leaves, shoots and fruit have a good natural resistance to both scab and mildew. The trees grow with moderate strength and usually crop well, though some growers complain of a tendency to biennial bearing. Like Worcester, Fortune has some slight resistance to frost after flowering. A minor failing is that Fortune's young sappy shoots seem to be rather slow to lignify, so that early in the season they are unusually attractive to twig-cutting weevils and later on are often snapped off short by wind; the ill-timed pruning by these long-snouted, iridescent little weevils sometimes makes it difficult to form a shapely tree. The language of apple flavour is so deficient that Fortune, after achieving sweetness, juiciness and good texture in its crisp yet soft, yellowish flesh, can only be said to be of excellent quality with a full aromatic flavour. Fortune, conical in shape and a little ribbed round the eye, should finish to a good golden yellow with a red cheek and scarlet stripes; sometimes it fails to – and a green September dessert apple has no prospects – but it is a variety that usually answers well to pre-harvest hormone spraying, which allows the full colour to develop. Fortune can easily come too small, and needs some thinning in most seasons; it appears to be a variety which needs generous manurial treatment. Little is yet known of its behaviour in cold or gas store; it can be sold from the trees, or from barn store until late October. It does well in the north and keeps longer; in Scotland they call it a Christmas apple.

Of other September apples, James Grieve, such a martyr to scab and canker, used to be grown particularly as a pollinator for Cox, because of its unfailing and abundant blossom. When fully ripe it is excellent but so prone to bruising that it is usually marketed hard and green, when nobody wants it; it retires to the garden whence it came. Two new varieties are Taunton Cross, from Long Ashton Research Station, well liked in the west, scab proof, but nothing particular in either appearance or flavour, and Merton Worcester, from John Innes Horticultural Insti-

tution, a Cox × Worcester cross. Merton Worcester closely
follows Worcester proper in picking and keeps longer. It
could sometimes pass as Cox in appearance, and may yet
come to do so on street barrows. Merton Worcester's
orchard performance appears to be all that it should, the
trees are healthy, blossom freely, and the attractive-
looking fruit, touched with russet as a good English apple
should be, is very juicy and sweet and has some quality
as well. It has not been long enough on trial for anything
more than a 'shows promise' judgement.

Mid-Season Dessert Apples.—The variety chosen in the
National Fruit Trials as the mid-season standard variety
is Ellison's Orange, well known for biennial bearing and
for its flavour of aniseed. It is not a bad little pippin, with
a useful degree of frost resistance, but is hardly planted
now. This habit of biennial bearing, which is such a shortcoming in several other orchard varieties, such as Miller's
Seedling and Laxton's Superb, is a genetical character,
which usually gets worse as the trees grow older. But regular
bearing varieties can also be thrown into biennialism by
starvation and over-cropping, and by spring frosts. It is a
character that exists in various degrees and can partly be
overcome by clever pruning or by drastic blossom thinning
– removing 75 per cent of the blossom – at the beginning of
an 'on' year. Growers with established trees of biennial
varieties have no choice but to go on with them, but there
is no need to continue planting such varieties when there
is a choice of as good, or better, regular bearers.

Ellison's Orange is likely to be replaced as the standard
mid-season dessert by yet another of Laxton's introductions,
Lord Lambourne, a Worcester × James Grieve cross.
Mention of Lambourne immediately introduces the subject
of virus, for Lambourne alone can almost be said to have
founded the study of virus diseases in apples. Viruses have
disastrously run through the soft fruit industry, leaving
a fearful train of bonfires (there is no other cure) and neces-
sitating the introduction of government certification of
nursery stocks, so that only clean material is planted. Now

it is the turn of tree fruits: Stunt in plums, Stony Pit in
pears, Rasp Leaf, Rusty Mottle, Tatter Leaf and many
more in cherries; the unnatural distortions among apples,
so well displayed by Lambourne, are named Chat Fruit,
Rubbery Wood, Mosaic and Flat Limb. A tree of Lambourne grows normally until it crops, then all the apples
turn out to be miserable little green runts the size of plums
– this is Chat Fruit. There is a remedy, apart from the bonfire, because surprisingly enough it is safe to graft most
other varieties on to infected Lambourne; even the Rubbery
Wood virus, where the shoots fail to lignify and remain
as pliable as a basket maker's willow, is not usually
transmitted when infected trees are worked over to another
variety. If left alone Rubbery Wood Lambournes go into a
drooping and unfruitful decline, and the older wood has
an unpleasant flexibility, like a rubber hose pipe. Chat
Fruit and Rubbery Wood are often associated, sometimes
with the distorted branches of Flat Limb as well.

The names alone given to these viruses show what a
short way research and knowledge have got; they have
an early nineteenth century flavour, as when the attacks
of all sorts of unidentified pests and diseases used to be
lumped together as The Blight. Those were the days when
fruit varieties were supposed to be strictly limited in life
span and to die eventually of old age; now it seems more
likely that when gradual decline in vigour, disease resistance and cropping does occur in a variety, it may be due
to progressive virus infection. No doubt virus in tree fruits
will be worse before it is better, and probably a good deal
of poor tree performance, now put down to other causes,
will turn out to be due to combinations of virus infections.
Unfortunately some rootstocks in commercial stoolbeds
are now known to be infected with viruses that reveal no
symptoms, and only declare themselves when worked
with a susceptible indicator variety, like Lambourne. The
long term solution is the testing and issue by the research
stations of new virus-free clones of both rootstocks and
scion varieties, as has been done with soft fruits; a start

with tree fruits has already been made. Lambourne started clean but susceptible; it has got into its present state by being worked on to infected nursery rootstocks or by being top grafted in the orchard on to other varieties which are symptomless carriers of the diseases.

Meanwhile, why plant Lambourne? The answer is that clean stocks do exist and that Lambourne has valuable qualities, though of the sort to attract large rather than small scale growers. The apples are brilliantly beautiful and maintain a wonderfully even run of size and shape, so that they almost grade themselves; quality is nothing special beyond a crisp and juicy sweetness and the fruit has a greasy skin which collects dirt. The trees are smothered in blossom every year yet the fruitlets generally thin themselves to a crop that the trees can bring to a good size; they strike their own balance of growth and crop, and their regular performance has given the variety a reputation as a rent payer.

Lambourne is the only promising newcomer among mid season apples. Established varieties of which a commercial acreage exists, but which have had their day as far as new planting is concerned, are such as Charles Ross, too big and soon going woolly; Allington Pippin, 'awkward Allington,' so subject to distressing lenticel spot and really too brisk for modern taste where sweetness is all, yet giving a wonderful flavour in an apple pie; and Rival, with its carmine bloom often hiding a peculiar glassy texture known as water core — no end to the fund of failings available, and orchard practice soon searches out every varietal weakness.

Winter Dessert Apples.—Only a narrow season is left for varieties that follow Worcester, before oncoming Cox swamps everything else. As a commercial apple Cox is a comparative beginner, and until quite recently was thought a great gamble. Yet whatever the opinions of the past, Cox can be a heavy and regular cropper, when exactly suited by soil and site, rootstock and management. Cox has gone all over the world and yet, luckily for home growers, seems able to give of its best not much more than a hundred miles from its old home at Colnbrook. Even imported Cox, which has no more sea to cross than the Channel, is recognizably a different apple. Continental Cox's are generally shinier, more streaky and less russeted than English, and so far English grown Cox has commanded a premium over imported.

Cox in the orchard makes a rather dense and twiggy tree, soon becoming weak and straggling if not well done; it is a variety that cannot miss careful annual pruning. When lightly pruned, Cox readily makes blossom buds on two- and three-year-old wood and goes on to carry fruit in perfect ropes, like strings of onions — a wealthy sight. Cox seldom needs thinning, which is not to say that it never has enough apples, but rather that it can bring off a heavy crop without losing much size. When fully protected Cox trees grow and crop healthily, but have no natural resistance whatever to any of the pests and diseases that so well support the spray chemical industry, and moreover they are unusually susceptible to spray damage; 'unsafe on Cox' is the commonest of manufacturers' directives. Cox also shows a peculiarity of its own, 'Cox spot,' which consists of small, brown, dead areas in the leaf but which appears to be harmless, except for reducing the effective area of the leaf. Cox is among the most sensitive of all apples to spring frost damage, and, having survived that season, usually shows more 'June drop' of the fruitlets than other varieties. In too wet a soil Cox collapses with canker, in too dry it is ravaged by red spider; if rainfall is too high scab is uncontrollable, and if the summer climate is too cold and grey the trees will not crop. If the spring is cold the apples are cracked and coarsely russeted, if the summer is too hot they scald; in a late summer mixture of drought and thunderstorms the skin hardens in drought and then bursts open when the rain comes.

Cox has succeeded on many different soils, but from all of them it demands perfect drainage, either natural or contrived, and a good humus content. A thirty-inch rainfall is quite enough for Cox and it soon feels any lack of summer sun or warmth; hopeless in the north. It has disappointed many growers, but few can afford to give it up.

From time to time bud sports appear in apple varieties; the 'sported' bud grows into a branch and bears fruit which is slightly different from the rest, being often redder. Usually it is only the brighter colour which attracts attention and such coloured sports have often been propagated, such as Red Melba, already mentioned, Redcoat Grieve, and there is even a Crimson Bramley. Among Cox sports, Crimson Cox has long been known, but it is an unattractive, very dark colour. Cherry Cox, brought over from the Continent, is the latest and is said to keep longer, but again it is much too dark. Cox should look lovely in its own right, with its red flush and yellowy gold touched with native russet; too often much of the English crop is green which accounts for the search – mistaken, as I think – for brighter coloured sports.

Cox above all varieties has been used by apple breeders, in fact hardly a cross is made nowadays without Cox, or an earlier child of Cox, being one of the parents. Cox has fathered or mothered many good quality apples yet so far it has always held back its own highly characteristic aroma, 'bite' and effervescence. There is no sign of anything to supersede Cox, and the only reason for growing anything else of its season is when Cox itself is unsatisfactory. Sunset is such a Cox replacement, less demanding in every way and now becoming popular. Sunset is a rather small flat apple which can be exceedingly pretty in golden yellow and bright light red, which grows and crops freely, and is of excellent quality. Unfortunately its colour, which should be its strong point, is not always forthcoming, and it is a borderline case for size.

Why not Blenheim Orange, or Ribston Pippin, the great apples of the nineteenth century? They are hardly planted now, yet are still well known and admired, particularly at Christmas time. Ribston is no easier than Cox, and in spite of its undeniable quality is rather too dry for modern taste — the Victorians' connoisseurship of port wine and nuts and dessert apples, their savouring of the old spicy, dry, yellow fleshed varieties, has been replaced by the crude modern liking for sugar and juiciness above all. Blenheim is difficult too; an extremely strong grower and very slow to crop; too liable to canker and scab; the fruit often too large and ugly — the beautiful Blenheim rosy pastel colour comes from old half-starved trees in grass; the flavour, in spite of the remarkable Blenheim nuttiness, often too acid; an exceptional apple but not exceptional enough.

In natural store Cox does not keep reliably much beyond Christmas and from light sandy soils hardly till then; in gas store it lasts into March. Some growers are not particularly bothered about finding an apple to follow Cox, though everyone agrees on the urgency of finding a better first early than Bath. They like to see their apple crop cleared at Christmas, leaving the New Year free for orchard work. They may not be able to continue so easily. The longer the season of home-grown fruit and the greater the proportion of home-grown against imported, the better the long-term prospects for the industry. At present the season from January to March or April is largely supplied by imported fruit, and it ought to be home grown. Larger growers may be happy with their gas-stored Cox, Worcester and Superb, but those working a small acreage with limited capital can hardly afford to disregard the back end of the season.

At present there is no accepted standard variety to follow Cox. Laxton's Superb nearly achieves the position and comes third to Cox and Worcester in annual tonnage, but, although it stores well, its natural season lasts barely into February, and it has many shortcomings. Superb's reputarion rose very fast – it was only introduced in 1918, from a Cox × Wyken Pippin cross – and was going to be the late red apple so long sought; it was the greatest introduction since Cox, and so on, but it is showing signs of declining as fast as it rose. It has a list of defects longer than that of any other commercial variety. Superb is obstinately biennial, getting worse with age, though its 'on' season crops are so heavy that it often averages a greater weight per acre over the years than any other dessert variety; the trees' strong yet willowy, whippy habit is awkward; they will not stand drought; the fruit from young trees is coarse, ill finished and over-large — a general rule with the first few crops of most varieties, but unusually marked with Superb. The fruit on the tree is badly subject to brown rot – a grave error in any apple and most of all in a late-keeper – so that in a warm wet autumn brown rot can run through an orchard with epidemic speed and halve the crop; this is bad enough, but the rot often spreads back into bark and wood. Superb's colour is often muddy, instead of a good though never very bright red; its white flesh is juicy and sweet and not much more. On the credit side Superb shows resistance to apple canker, which makes it popular in the wet west, and the fruit has the advantage of being saleable in September, as well as hanging, storing and travelling well. I think a new, small acreage grower would make a mistake in planting Superb.

The most promising candidate for Superb's place is Bowden's Seedling, an apple of peculiar origin. It came to the National Fruit Trials from Torquay of all places where Mr Bowden was a nurseryman, and had the reputed parentage Cox × Cornish Aromatic. It turned out to be almost indistinguishable from well known Jonathan, but of better flavour and more regular shape than imported fruit. Jonathan is one of the rare apples that when self-pollinated comes more or less true from seed; it seems most likely that Mr Bowden got his pips mixed and raised such a seedling. The few growers who already have bearing trees sell the fruit as English grown Jonathan. The outstanding merits of Bowden's Seedling are its very heavy and regular bearing and its brilliant light colour — the apples are bright shining red all over. A firm resistance to scab and the ability, like Lambourne, to do its own thinning, are other creditable characters. The original Jonathan from North America was tried many years ago by one or two large growers and was then found wanting – the fruit was too small and did not colour well – but it is being tried again, particularly at East Malling, where young trees have borne heavy crops of brilliant colour and good size without difficulty.

Bowden's Seedling and Jonathan have two weaknesses, a liability of the young shoots to powdery mildew – which can be controlled by rather painstaking pruning and by extra doses of lime sulphur – and a peculiarity of the fruit called 'Jonathan spot.' This appears as tiny sunken spots in the skin, and usually develops towards the end of the apples' storage life. Sometimes it appears sooner and seems to be associated with too early picking, as other varieties occasionally show similar symptoms; apples do have their seasons and commercial growers cannot always get away with treating them like potatoes.

Jonathan (and Bowden's Seedling, for the trees are indistinguishable) comes in nicely for picking after Cox, the fruit hangs splendidly and can be left even into the beginning of November. The trees share an interesting characteristic with a few other varieties, the habit of regularly and freely making blossom buds along one-year-old wood. Such buds open a week or ten days later than normal buds of two- and three-year-old wood and of spurs, and do not normally set fruit. But should the normal blossom be wiped out by frost, the later flowers do set a crop. This idiosyncrasy might be extremely valuable now and then, though fruit from blossoms on one-year-old wood is always smaller than normal. Quality is nothing special, though English grown fruit has the same abundant sweetness for which imported Jonathan is so well known. The future of the variety is questionable, as its natural storage life is hardly longer than that of Cox; though picked later, it is a supplementer rather than an extender of the Cox season, an awkward position for any apple to be in. Jonathan, however, does cold store safely until late March, and English grown fruit has then lately made the highest prices of any variety except Cox. Two other late-keeping varieties, Merton

Prolific from the John Innes Horticultural Institution, and Cortland, from the New York State Agricultural Experiment Station, are both fairly promising but have not yet been under trial for long enough.

Early Spring Dessert Apples.—The very late varieties, whose planting so far has been more or less experimental, are in a different class. These select few – Winston, Tydeman's Late Orange, Granny Smith and Wagener – are apples which keep with little loss in natural store until March or even April. It may seem shocking that popular nonenities like Jonathan from North America and Granny Smith from Australia should now be entering English orchards, where all used to be spice and character, but the public pays good money for them when imported, and they are at least sweet. He is a brave man who sets out to teach the public what they ought to like.

Of the four very late varieties the most planted is Winston, once called Winter King and supposed to be a result of that common but uninspired cross, Worcester × Cox. Winston however has one grave defect; it is too small, and can be grown big enough only with a struggle. Yet its other qualities are so good, and indeed endearing, that it cannot be dismissed. In orchard and in store Winston is as near foolproof as any commercial apple is likely to be. The trees are remarkably stiff and upright, which makes them difficult to prune, and they bear heavy crops, even after drastic thinning, with great regularity. Winston's chief competitor is Tydeman's Late Orange, a Cox × Superb cross recently distributed from East Malling and at the 'shows promise' stage. The trouble with Late Orange is its appearance, much of the skin often being covered with russet that looks like sandpaper, and I have seen samples looking as if they had been dipped in liquid mud; the rather dull red cheek brightens up in store, but the general look of a boxful is undeniably rough. However some much better looking samples have been grown in Essex.

Late Orange takes after its parent Superb in vigour and in tiresome whippiness of growth but much worse, a weak-

c

ness for brown rot has come through as well. I have rows of Winston and Late Orange growing alongside each other, and their differences are remarkable to follow through the season. Late Orange, loose and lax; Winston, stiff and upright; off they go in the spring, covered with blossom, setting a mass of fruitlets and carrying on into summer without incident. Scab is easily controlled on both of them. Then in an August heatwave Late Orange sun-scalds, some of the apples look as if they had been fried on one side; Winston is unaffected. A thunderstorm comes and some Late Orange split open; Winston unaffected. Bird pecking begins, two months or more before picking time, and Late Orange collapses with brown rot, each peck or split a focus of infection which spreads to any sound apple within reach and then back into the spurs. Pecks on Winston dry up, nine times out of ten. Both crops survive autumn gales. At picking time, at the end of October or early November, both crops hang tightly to the nearly leafless trees, Late Orange, mahogany and sandpaper, Winston, tough skinned, bright shining red. Unless heavily thinned in the summer both varieties have a high proportion of 'smalls,' and the average size of the fruit is also likely to be too small. In barn store both varieties endure with little loss until well into March; Late Orange brightens its red and warms its grey russet, Winston's green base colour turns to yellow. Both are of good dessert quality, the firm yellow flesh of Late Orange sometimes a little dry, but both sweet and acid, with a rich flavour of real character; while Winston, strongly scented, has juicy white flesh tinged with green, sweet, but with a slightly bitter undertone.

These two were the best of twenty varieties tested over three seasons at the Ditton Laboratory for cold storage behaviour and for dessert quality (*The Storage Qualities of Late Dessert Varieties of Apples*, HMSO, 1952). The Tasting Panel's adjudication at monthly intervals never dropped below 'good' from early January to the end of March, as long as the fruit tested had not been picked before late October. Both varieties were assessed as 'very good' on occasion and Winston reached 'excellent.' (The grades were excellent, very good, good, fair, poor, very poor). The ugly old Essex apple D'Arcy Spice was the only other variety to get either of these marks, except that after the hot summer of 1947 Orleans Reinette was 'very good' in January (with 28 per cent wastage) and Belle de Boskoop 'excellent' in March. None of these three can be called commercial varieties. Storage temperatures were 31·5°F and 37°F; the wastage by rotting from January to March was generally negligible in both Late Orange and Winston, and neither showed any scald or physiological breakdown. Early and late picking compared showed that colour, quality and size were all much improved by leaving the fruit on the trees as long as possible, but that storage life was slightly shortened.

The cold storage behaviour of Granny Smith and of Wagener, an eighteenth century variety from North America, was very different. Both are known to keep excellently in barn or shed store until April, without loss or shrivelling, but in a cold storage trial at 37°F Granny Smith simply failed to ripen, was classed as 'fair' in January and February – inferior to imported fruit – and by March was really nasty; yet there was no wastage whatever by mid-April. Fruit taken in mid-April from the 31·5°F chamber, in an attempt to ripen it at 54°F, simply collapsed. Wagener turned out to be damaged by a temperature of 37°F and started breaking down in January; its flavour then or later was never better than 'fair to good.' It seems that both these varieties, which originated in hot summer countries, cannot ripen fully in English summers and if stopped short by being clapped into cold store, never come to anything. Evidently in the higher temperatures of barn stores they go on ripening very slowly and end up in much better condition. Both varieties need to be left on the trees until mid-November, where they hang indifferent to the weather.

The fruit of both Granny Smith and Wagener sells well

enough in April and both varieties are being tried by a few growers. Trees of Wagener are even more like Lombardy poplars than Winston; they crop heavily but incline to biennialism. Wagener is all but scab-proof, but is rather liable to mildew. The apples are flat and rather uneven in shape, medium sized, sometimes ripening to no more than a stripey yellowy-green, sometimes to a bright red and yellow; they have a strong smell and taste soapy. Granny Smith is characteristically as hard as a bullet and green as grass, being among dessert apples the exception that proves the rule; its quality can be better than Wagener and the trees grow and crop freely.

So much for the dessert apples of English orchards; if they sound like a collection of chronic invalids it is only another way of saying that preventative spraying is the most important single operation in commercial apple growing.

Cooking Apples.—Among cooking apples it is Bramley all the way, a single variety almost as commonplace and universal a commodity as potatoes, with a season nearly as long. Bramley stores wonderfully well and in gas chambers keeps even into June. Lately the markets have started demanding the first of the new crop in August — August for a cooker whose proper season is November to March. That is the modern way: find some really reliable article, mass produce it, and extend it beyond its proper limits without regard for quality.

Cooking apples used to be much more of a farmer's than a specialized grower's crop than they are now, and the chief reason is their increasing demands on spraying. Bramley started life in the 'eighteen-seventies as a scab-free variety and long remained clean, but now it is as bad as any. It was all very well in the old days for a mixed farmer to have a block of Bramleys; it is a different matter now, with a contractor having to come in for winter washing and three or four times later for lime sulphur spraying. The big trees need a big machine which could never pay its way on a few acres; and Bramley always makes a big tree.

Although so universal, Bramley is far from perfect, being well known for unusual sensitivity to frost before blossoming and for bearing fruit not as well-shaped as it might be. Bramley has virtually no competitors at present, though two other late cookers are worth consideration, the old established Edward VII and the newcomer Howgate Wonder. Edward VII, a neat upright tree, flowers very late and lack of pollination may account for a reputation for light cropping in some districts. The attractions are its freedom from scab and its beautiful, large and round, even-shaped fruits that slowly turn from grass green to pale yellow. They keep until April. Howgate Wonder has the virtues of producing large, or enormous, well-shaped fruit with no smalls and of being able to carry a parthenocarpic crop in a frosty year, i.e., a crop of seedless apples produced without pollination. Early and mid-season cookers are not likely to attract a new grower nowadays. Arthur Turner makes early size and is better than the standard early cooker, Emneth Early; and in mid-season the standard Grenadier is challenged by George Neal and Sowman's Seedling. Monarch is a long season, red and white cooking apple, sometimes sold in the north for dessert, and fairly widely planted in the eastern counties; its failing is brittleness of wood which makes the propping of laden branches essential.

Whatever varieties are finally chosen to start a new plantation, it is well to plant a little museum at the same time, and to keep adding to it. Apples vary widely according to soil and site, and a variety can be useless on one's own ground, however successful elsewhere. It is as well to have an idea of how a brand-new variety will perform under one's own conditions before planting it on any scale. Also, the grafting-over of discarded varieties in established orchards is becoming a more common practice, and a new grower should have an idea of what to try next if any of the present-day commercial varieties fail to earn their keep, or if any little gamble with an unproved or unknown variety does not come off.

Rootstocks.—The great majority of bush dessert apples

in commercial orchards are supported by a rootstock known as East Malling Type II. The choice of rootstocks is much narrower than that of scion varieties, but is almost as vital; the root system is the greater part of a tree. The confusion which formerly existed in the naming and performance of vegetatively reproduced rootstocks, the medley of old 'doucin' or 'paradise' stocks, has been sorted out by nearly forty years' work at East Malling, resulting in the selected Malling series, which are now always known by number, and which give a greater range of tree size than is available in any other fruit.

Type II (M II) has made its reputation by all-round reliability in a variety of soils and conditions. Trees on it crop heavily fairly early in their lives and grow vigorously. Under modern conditions apple trees are encouraged to grow more freely and loosely than formerly and it is now reckoned that in good soils mature trees of dessert varieties on Type II need a spacing of 24 ft. apart. Type I, the old Broad-leafed English Paradise rootstock, is of similar vigour and, though better anchored than II, is less adaptable and sometimes makes an unthrifty tree, particularly with Cox; it does better on the moister soils, but its use is gradually decreasing. These two are classed as vigorous rootstocks. For smaller trees the only genuinely semi-dwarfing rootstock is Type VII, which needs an 18 ft. spacing where Type II needs 24 ft. It grows vigorously enough at the start to make a decent tree, and at all stages crops heavily for its size. Type VII is rather liable to throw suckers, and its roots often grow unsightly galls, of bacterial origin, though this does not seem to affect the trees' performance. Trees of ultimate size between those on II and VII are grown by Type IV, Holstein or Dutch Doucin, a rootstock that might have become leader of all if it were not for its fatal weakness of bad anchorage. Type IV needs a stake all its life, and a fence post at that, yet its weak and spreading root system resists drought better than Type II. Many heavily bearing Continental orchards are on Type IV, and over twenty-five years at East Malling it induced handsomely the heaviest crops of all rootstocks tested. Some wonderful crops of Cox have been grown on Type IV and this is probably the only use for it nowadays.

For really dwarf apple bushes there is nothing except Type IX, and a good many growers wish they had never set eyes on it. It is a wonderful rootstock all the same, though, apart from its place in gardens, it is essentially a smallholder's stock for the semi-intensive growing of high quality dessert apples only. Trees on Type IX can never be ranched; they demand first rate soil conditions and generous treatment, freedom from weed competition, careful annual pruning, and a lifelong stake. Inadequately staked, or unstaked trees on IX readily blow over, which is easily corrected, but they are as likely to snap off at ground level, which is not. Type IX donates a lax and spreading habit, and the branches usually need some tying up towards harvest, for the weight of fruit can break the little trees to pieces. More than any other rootstock IX induces precocious bearing; apples are borne on Type IX trees when they are still the size of pot plants. This is a disadvantage rather than an advantage, for a framework has to be built up before the precocious crops can have any significance. Type IX simply has not the strength to grow vigorously and crop heavily. Under unfavourable conditions the trees remain poor little runts, but on good land Cox on IX should have made a nice little tree at five years from planting, 6 ft. high and through, and bearing heavily.

Dessert apples usually give their best colour on Type IX, probably due to their better exposure to sunlight rather than to a direct rootstock effect, but even more important, fruit size is consistently and significantly increased. Type IX is supposed to donate a degree of scab resistance to varieties worked on to it but this awaits experimental demonstration on a statistical basis. The little trees can never give more than a bushel of fruit, and have to be closely planted to compare with the four or five bushels sometimes given by Type II trees; a spacing of 12 ft. is usually about right for them. Type IX trees have often been used as

temporary fillers in a young orchard but they have as good
an expectation of profitable life as the more vigorous
Malling rootstocks.

These Malling stocks, Types IX, VII, IV and II are the
only ones likely to interest a new planter on a limited
acreage. Types XII, XVI, XXV, and Crab C, as well as
seedling rootstocks, are used for standard and half standard
trees, suitable for apple ranches but not for small scale
intensive plantations.

Type II would probably go on indefinitely as the standard
bush tree rootstock if it were not for the new Malling-
Merton series, now entering commerce, and the first range
of deliberately bred rootstocks to do so. The MM stocks
are all resistant to Woolly Aphid, though this character
is more pertinent in Commonwealth countries than in
England, and they cover a similar range of vigour to that
of the Malling series. The most outstanding of the new series
seems to be MM 104 and if I were starting apple planting
again and was in no great hurry I should want to wait a
year or two until I could get trees on this stock. MM 104
combines the very heavy and precocious cropping of M IV
with an anchorage which has no equal in the Malling series;
it may be possible for trees to be grown on it unstaked
throughout their lives. If MM 104 turns out to be all that
it promises after nine years' trial – which is all that trees
worked on any of the MM series have yet had (1945–54) –
it may bring about quite a revolution in dessert apple
orchards by increasing yields and cheapening costs. At
nine years old trees on MM 104 are slightly smaller than
the same varieties on M II.

There is no substitute for M IX in the Malling-Merton
series so far introduced, but M VII seems likely to be replaced by MM 106, donating similar vigour and cropping,
but not given to either suckers or galls. On poor sandy
soils where an intensive plantation is wanted MM 106
seems a useful substitute for M IX, and under such conditions makes a smaller tree than M VII. Reliable M II
is challenged by MM 109, of similar yield and anchorage

but rather larger and more drought resistant, and by MM 111 of similar size, but so far nearly up to M IV in its cropping.

These are the rootstocks and the scion varieties that, married just above soil level, make the grower's raw material. At present Cox and Type II are his most constant companions; Cox no doubt will stay, but its root system seems ready to change.

Chapter Three

DESIGNING AN APPLE PLANTATION

THE expectation of life of an apple plantation is much the same as mankind's three score years and ten, and in the course of both there is room for many errors, some redeemable, some not. The fact that one crop will occupy a field for a lifetime shows how extremely inflexible is tree-fruit growing compared to other branches of farming, and when starting from an empty field the necessity of the planter being also a prophet is obvious. When a new orchard is still at the beginning of its useful life ten years will have passed. Planning a new plantation is like having to design a 1960 model car in 1950. Much must remain a matter for speculation and guesswork, but a firm body of knowledge about fruit growing is now available; there is changing fashion but also there is basic knowledge, and many glaring mistakes of the past need not be made again.

There are many considerations before an orchard can be planned on squared paper. This in fact comes last. First of all, site and soil must be right, water must be available, labour allowed for, the scale of orcharding decided on; the coat must be cut according to the cloth.

Sites and Soils.—The climatic and soil conditions required by apple trees are well understood, and though there is nothing magical about 'fruit land' several strict conditions have to be fulfilled. The site must be relatively free from spring frosts, about whose behaviour there is nothing difficult, though it is only recently a matter of general knowledge. In a radiation frost the cold air formed at ground level, by heat loss from earth to sky, flows downhill like water, though much more slowly and stickily. The cold air fills up enclosed hollows, sometimes to great depth, and any obstruction across a slope, such as a hedge, acts as a dam and builds a pond of cold air above it. It is a matter of relative topography; frosty hollows can occur equally well at 500 ft. or 50. On a flat plain, where the cold air must lie where it is formed, a depth of 10 ft. of air below freezing point can be built up in a long lasting spring frost. An ideal orchard site lies on a gentle slope, a two-way slope if possible, with free air drainage below it, and as little cold air as possible flowing down from above.

Some fruit farms have been planted on hilltops to avoid radiation frosts, but the wind frosts they then catch can be just as damaging; and, short of frost, cold north and east winds at blossom time keep insects at home when they might be busy pollinating. Exposed orchards can also be much damaged by late summer and autumn gales and their spraying routine interfered with in the spring. In a valley the fruit land is the slopes, not the crests and not the bottom. Aspect is of little importance as long as the slopes are gentle, for although the micro-climates of different aspects do differ, the effect is usually not large enough to matter. Steep slopes should be avoided like the plague, for every operation is made more troublesome and expensive; an old tractor on worn rubbers, perfectly adequate on level site, is useless and dangerous on a hillside. The soil is also uneven on steep banks, thin and poor on the brow, deep and rich from centuries of wash-off at the foot.

An elevation of 500 ft. is quite high enough for dessert apples, for increasing humidity towards cloud base makes scab control ever more difficult, and rainfall may become too high. Rainfall may also be too low in some districts, particularly on shallow or gravelly soils; the interest in extremely expensive irrigation schemes now shown by North Kent and Essex growers particularly is a sufficient pointer. An annual rainfall of rather more than 25 in. is better than rather less, especially as in some eastern districts rainfall has been running below average in recent years. A good supply of water from ponds or streams, or piped water, is essential, as under conventional spraying methods an acre of mature bush trees receives some 2,000 gallons a year. As for temperature, dessert apples like well-marked seasons. Mild wet autumns leading into warm winters, as in the south-west and extreme west, keep the trees growing too long so that the wood does not ripen properly. As for summer, as already mentioned, all the dessert apple districts have an average day temperature of 68°F or more in July and August, and of 64°F in September.

A perfect site is thus characterized by a gentle slope; there is a clear run for cold air below it and it is not too much frowned upon by higher land above; there is shelter from westerly gales in autumn and from cold east winds in spring; the rainfall is about 25 in., and there are plentiful water supplies at hand.

Big elms, old hawthorns and strong nettles are the traditional signs of a good fruit soil and are widespread enough to show that tree fruits succeed on a variety of soils. The qualities they are supposed to signify are: elms, depth of soil; hawthorns, perfect drainage; and nettles, available nitrates. Beech is an indicator of free drainage, coltsfoot of the opposite, usually on heavy clay. Rushes of course are an elementary sign of water near the surface and sometimes occur in upland clays, which merely means that they need draining. Horsetail often means the existence of an impermeable 'pan.' Fathen is characteristic of arable soils rich in organic matter; its alternative name, dungweed, says as much. Sorrell is a sure sign of acidity.

There are successful apple orchards on loams, sands, gravels, clays and on soils consisting mostly of stones. Texture, depth and drainage are far more important than natural richness, for plant nutrients can be supplied as they are required. These are the qualities that have made the brick earths so famous, with their beautiful silky feel. They remain the prime apple soils, but generally exist only in small patches and even so are no more than deep, consistent loams, with the fractions of sand and clay nicely proportioned.

The amount of water still held by a soil after all the 'free' water has drained off is called its field capacity;

this varies from about 1 in. per foot of depth for sands to about 2 in. for clays. The pull on this reservoir by evaporation and by the transpiration of trees and cover crop generally handsomely exceeds rainfall throughout the growing season; a cumulative rainfall deficit, i.e. the difference between rainfall and total water loss from the soil, can easily reach 10 in. by August and can only be made up again during the winter when soil moisture will be restored to field capacity. Depth of soil available to apple roots is thus of great importance; grass browns in an August drought and clover stays green simply because the clover roots go down to levels where there is still a reserve of soil water. Even Type IX's roots can go down 10 ft. or more if the soil allows them to. It is generally held that a minimum depth of 2 ft. of root-worthy soil is necessary for dessert apples, and the more than this the better; a sandy soil is a practical proposition only if deep.

Winter waterlogging and summer droughting go together; roots must have air as well as water and roots submerged below the water table in winter die of asphyxiation, so the living roots left above the water table are insufficient and work in an insufficient volume of soil to carry the tree through a subsequent summer drought. Thus comes about the seeming paradox of water causing drought. In any apple soil the winter water table has to be below the root range. A water table near the surface often means an impervious layer in the subsoil, often a pan in gravelly and sandy soils or a clay so dense and obdurate that water seepage is practically at a standstill. Any pan within range must be broken up by pulling a subsoiling tine through it, and a bad clay, with the characteristic mottling associated with impeded drainage, can only be made fit for orcharding by expensive pipe drainage. A pan a few inches deep is often formed when ploughing has been too often repeated at the same depth.

Before any planting is thought of, whether the land is already in hand or still in the market, it is absolutely essential for a new planter to have site and soil vetted by an expert, either through the NAAS or by a private fruit consultant, or both. The performance of dessert apples on different soil series is now well enough known for the results of planting a new site to be forecast with a good degree of reliability. Analyses of available potash and phosphate are required, estimation of pH, and percentage of organic matter. Apples are not choosy about pH, but marked acidity or alkalinity are unfavourable; a shade on the acid side of neutrality is ideal. Deficiency of organic matter can be corrected without much difficulty, apart from time and expense; a content of much below 10 per cent needs urgent treatment.

Some of the rules are sometimes deliberately flaunted. Cooking apples grow and crop so well in the deep rich soils often associated with frosty bottoms that it may be worth losing perhaps one crop in five. But when unsuitable soils have been planted success is sometimes more surprising than failure. No one could ever recommend planting apples on a thin soil over chalk, for instance, yet the colour and skin finish of fruit from such soils has to be seen to be believed; Blenheim rosy bright with a beautiful eggshell sheen, as unlike the usual dull russeted green as if it were a different variety. Chalk soils are not so impossible as they used to be, since the great trouble of chlorosis – chalk-induced iron deficiency – can be cured by injecting iron sulphate tablets into the tree stems (though some of the good colour may be due to iron deficiency). Grassing down is essential on a chalk soil, and the trees may give of their best only in a wet year. Certain varieties have the reputation of doing well on chalk, such as Newton Wonder, the big well-coloured cooker whose smaller fruits are justifiably sold for dessert in the spring, Charles Ross, Blenheim Orange, Barnack Beauty — a red and yellow late dessert, usually condemned by poor cropping but said to bear well on chalk. Unfortunately the flavour of chalk-grown apples does not seem to match their appearance. Sands also produce high colour, but early maturity; apples on a clay soil can hang nearly a month longer on the tree than the same variety on a light sand, and keep proportionately longer.

There is much to be said for establishing new plantations away from the recognized fruit areas, where land still available is likely to be either unsuitable or over-expensive. A reserve of pests and diseases is always ready in established fruit areas to spread with epidemic speed. Since the war new planting has moved particularly towards East Anglia in Essex and Suffolk. A huge block of central southern England – Berks, Bucks and Oxon, Hampshire and Wiltshire – awaits further development; the rainfall is right and there is wide choice of soil and site.

The Scale of Planting.—A prospective grower should decide the eventual scale of his planting from the beginning, whether the decision is free or forced, because type of tree, planting distances, varieties and required machinery all vary according to total acreage. Round about forty acres is usually thought to be the most practical size to give the working owner-manager a good living. The argument is that forty acres will justify full-scale modern machinery, but that half or even a quarter of the acreage will need the same equipment without justifying it. However, it is not so simple. Machinery carefully used by one man on a small acreage lasts a great deal longer, and second-hand machines may be serviceable. Besides, orchard machinery exists in a range of capacity, size and cost proportionate to acreage, tree-size and closeness of planting; and fruit-growing – somewhere between farming and forestry, with some gardening thrown in – involves large operations like pruning and picking, which remain hand-work on any scale. The limit of mechanization is soon reached and thereafter one man will be needed for every ten acres of mature apple trees, whatever the total size of the holding. However, as a general rule small holdings are undoubtedly economically less efficient than larger. This is partly due to lack of capital and partly to the obvious tendency for abler brains to gravitate to larger enterprises. There are exceptions and, as far as apple growing is concerned, the disparity can be reduced only if the risks of out and out specialization are taken and the method of growing the trees is strictly appropriate to the size of the plantation.

It seems to me that a small scale specialist apple grower must hold unfailingly to two axioms. The first is that only the most valuable and the best quality varieties can be grown; the smaller the acreage the more care each tree and each apple can expect, and the smaller the crops the more valuable they must be. The perspicacity of the general public and nothing else has turned Cox into a commercial variety, and I think new planters should have faith that the public will also recognize quality in less well known varieties. I should list Epicure, Fortune, Sunset, Winston and Late Orange as the only other current commercial varieties safely recognizable for quality.

The second axiom is that a small acreage means dwarf trees. The smaller the trees the handier they are to manage and the better the chance of producing brightly coloured crops of good-sized apples. Small trees are less demanding in machinery, though no less open to mechanization on the appropriate scale. Big trees on a small acreage mean that advantage cannot be taken of the niceties of pruning and thinning, and spraying becomes the same problem as that facing a general farmer with a small block of overgrown Bramleys. Any country resident wanting to pay the gardener's wages by growing an acre or two of apples could hardly do worse than plant his paddock with standard trees.

Choice of Varieties.—These two axioms lead to the vital decisions of choice of varieties and choice of rootstocks. Everything points to Cox, but with the tremendous acreage already in being is it safe to go on planting it? Some think yes, some no, and the usual result in present new planting is a compromise — a proportion of Cox. If one thing is obvious it is that Cox will remain the standard English dessert apple for as long as can be foreseen, as standard as Jaffa oranges or Deglet Nour dates, but Cox farms – i.e. Cox only with a minimum of pollinator trees – seems now too much of a gamble, with the risks of market added to the large enough risks of growing. The small grower really has little choice; he must produce the best and Cox is the acknowledged best. If continental growers keep planting Cox for the English market, home growers can only do the same, but try and do it better and take advantage of their smaller transport costs.

No one knows what the eventual limit of Cox consumption may be and the law of supply and demand has not begun to operate. Nothing like the gluts of unsaleable plums is yet known and all that has happened is that in some years at the height of the apple season less popular varieties and lower grades of Cox have been difficult to sell, or not worth marketing. The frequent market report, 'Only best grade desserts move at all freely' will soon become the rule. As the tonnage of Cox increases, so its season is bound to lengthen. More and more Cox can be expected to go into cold and gas stores, to be held later and later in spite of wastage. Bramley has already pioneered along this road and Cox will no doubt follow. The Cox season also begins earlier and earlier; the markets start crying out for Cox in mid-September, in the middle of the Worcester season; the fruit makes high prices and then the home grower is blamed for low quality. Perhaps we shall see some big growers putting their Worcesters into gas store for sale in February and selling their Cox's straight off the trees. Already there have been times when windfall Cox rushed to market after a September gale has made better money than graded, sized and wrapped fruit later in the season. However, from early land Cox can be more or less edible at the end of September. Type IX induces early maturity and gives the high colour that makes an unripe Cox look riper than it is. For a small grower not planning for an eventual cold store, Cox on Type IX seems a likely choice, particularly on early land.

Cox then remains an automatic choice but it would seem wise to hedge and not plant more than half the acreage to it. This is on marketing grounds, but considerations of

D

growing are just as important. Too much of one variety means a sudden army of pickers, and on a small scale the difference can easily be between having or having not to employ extra hands. Further, Cox has a high requirement for pollinators and two different pollinator varieties are better than one; a blossom failure in a solitary pollinator variety reduces the crop of both itself and of the main variety. So, spread the picking season by growing varieties maturing successively and at the same time spread the risk.

Mid-season Cox will be the first to be oversupplied and first to feel slowing sales and lowering prices. What of the position of Cox understudies and second strings? It would seem so obvious that a small grower planting Cox should not think of planting another variety of the same marketing season; surely the time will soon come when nothing but Cox is saleable in the Cox season —but will it? The present high prices for such as Jonathan, even equalling Cox at times, are surely a flash in the pan — or are they? When the shops are full of best Cox at 1s 3d and second grades at 9d, will there be room for a red doll apple at 1s? If so, the red doll's heavier crops - because only its colour and yield can keep it in business - will give a better return per acre. Cox after all is an adult taste, and many people and children like a sweet red apple if only for a change. The likeliest red doll is in fact Jonathan or Bowden's Seedling, but if they do not pay for extra care -- for the extra size and colour that can be got from dwarf trees - then they are best left to big growers.

The best choice of a variety to precede Cox seems to be Fortune, which fulfils the condition of being good enough to repay extra care. If Cox and Fortune are grown there is really no room left for October apples such as Lambourne; no gap in marketing, with Fortune ready from early September until Cox takes over in October, and no overlap in picking. If Winston is added, to take over from Cox after Christmas, the whole season from early September to March can be covered. Thus even if a small grower aims at keeping up uninterrupted local sales, no more than these three varieties are necessary, and with nothing better than ordinary barn storage. If only local sales are envisaged the number of trees of each variety should be in proportion to their season of marketing — in this case Fortune, $1\frac{1}{2}$ months (September and half October); Cox, $2\frac{1}{2}$ (second half October, November, December); Winston, 3 (January–March); three rows of Fortune to five of Cox to six of Winston.

Winston I should plant only on Type IX, or possibly on VII, because of the difficulty of getting it big enough and the necessity of thinning; the weakly drooping habit that Type IX encourages is also much braced by Winston's exceedingly stiff and upright branches. Winston does come a better size in the wet west country and is well thought of there, but still requires thinning because of its habit of setting fruitlets in clusters of four or five. It is well enough known to sell well but is never likely to become a national variety. It is such a good keeper that the slightly shorter storage life given by IX is no great matter.

Such a tiny number of varieties, which not long ago would have seemed a great risk, is now commonplace. The advantages of specialization are accepted and three carefully chosen varieties are enough to spread the risk, the harvesting and the marketing. Another reason for a small grower to keep to a minimum number of varieties is that it generally takes a consignment of at least a ton, or about fifty bushels to make the best price per bushel. Temptations like 'putting in a few Beauty of Bath to start the season' are much better resisted on a small place, and a small block of trees of a different variety soon turns out to be more trouble than it is worth.

Other varieties which might be worth their place on a small acreage are Epicure, but only if the holding is near a holiday centre, and Merton Worcester, being planted particularly in Essex to follow Worcester proper. No doubt other new varieties of merit are in existence and will emerge in a few years, but none have yet been sufficiently tested. Varieties like Worcester and Early Worcester, Lambourne and Laxton's Superb, Pearl, Michaelmas Red and John Standish – a brilliant turnip – I consider ranch apples unsuitable for small holdings or for growing as dwarf trees; they belong to big farms sending bulk loads to distant markets. Bowden's Seedling should belong with them on grounds of quality, and Sunset is in the even more precarious position of being an apple of quality and beauty – whose full colour is sometimes not forthcoming – of just before and during the Cox season; yet it has made a reputation.

Cooking apples are unlikely to interest a new planter on a small scale. There is a current argument that new planting of cookers is no longer keeping pace with grubbing, that in a few years many more Bramley orchards will become uneconomic through old age, decreasing quality and size of fruit, and that supplies may fall below demand. Certainly cookers are a staple and do not suffer from foreign competition, but they are essentially a big acreage crop — big trees, big machines, big stores; a low profit margin but a big turnover. In any case small scale plantings of cookers had better try for something different, Edward VII or Howgate Wonder perhaps.

People who want to risk being different may find the short list of varieties too drably commercial, may even take a sweeping decision and say 'All these commercial apples are going to be hopelessly overdone at home and abroad by the time anything I plant comes into full bearing. Only big highly capitalized growers will be able to keep going. I shall gamble on something entirely different and go for old English spicy high flavour.' (But the trouble with old English high flavour is that is is apt to be outclassed by such as Fortune, Cox and Sunset.) The likeliest choice for a gamble of this sort may be the Russets, which at least have the advantage of being generally highly scab resistant. They are traditionally welcome at Christmas time and can look quite inviting or dreadfully muddy. The most likely ones are St Edmund's Russet, September–October, brightest of all and of good flavour; Egremont Russet, just until Christmas, the best known and a good pollinator for Cox; and Brownlee's Russet, from January onwards. The interesting list of apples 'recommended for flavour' in the Royal Horticultural Society's *Select List of Hardy Fruits for Private Gardens* includes three current commercial varieties, Cox, Fortune and Epicure. Except for Laxton's Advance, the others are all old varieties: St Edmund's and Egremont Russets, Mother (USA), Gravenstein (Germany), Margil, Ribston, Orleans Reinette (?Holland), Ashmead's Kernel, Claygate Pearmain, Duke of Devonshire, and D'Arcy Spice. D'Arcy Spice is a good example of a totally uncommercial apple, biennial and impossibly ugly, yet still just grown commercially in Essex, where it is easily sold locally; it is an Essex apple and always said not to succeed outside East Anglia. Orleans Reinette, rather dry and like a smaller, flatter and brightened-up Blenheim, has been tried commercially in a small way. Edward Bunyard, whose *Anatomy of Dessert* should be known to any uncommercially minded grower, considered it 'the best apple grown in Western Europe.'

Pollination.—A few apple varieties are fully self-fertile, i.e. capable of setting a full crop with their own pollen, such as Worcester and Superb, but most require the pollen from another variety. Some are partly self-fertile, some not at all. Any varieties required to pollinate each other must flower at approximately the same time and have inter-fertile pollen. Apples are classed, according to their chromosome count, as diploids and triploids. The cytology need not be explained; the practical result is that diploids fertilize each other (if their blossoming overlaps), though some varieties have a higher percentage of viable pollen than others, but triploid pollen is largely infertile. All accepted commercial varieties so far mentioned are diploids, with the triploid exceptions of Bramley, Ribston and Blenheim. Blocks of Bramley only are just self-fertile enough, even with their 'bad' pollen, to set a full crop under ideal conditions, but better and more consistent crops are picked when a diploid companion is interplanted. And if the diploid is not fully self-fertile a third variety is necessary to pollinate it, since

Bramley pollen is unreliable. The most promising dessert apples for present planting all make good enough pollination companions in nearly any combination and their blossoming times overlap well enough. Apple flowering varies much in time from year to year, but the varieties usually faithfully maintain the same relative order. Numerous crosses amongst new and old varieties have been carried out by the National Fruit Trials to investigate compatibility for pollination, and flowering periods have been recorded and compared. The latest report of results, by the Director of the Trials, Mr J.M.S. Potter, appeared in the *Journal of the Royal Horticultural Society*, Vol. LXXVI, Part 8 (August, 1951). As for the means of pollination, some growers keep bees, some pay beekeepers to put their hives into the orchards at blossom time, and some do neither. Whether the population of wild insects, and of other people's bees, is adequate for pollination depends on size of orchard and on district. On a small scale it is reasonable to do without bees for as long as crops remain satisfactory, but when a poor set of fruit can be ascribed to no other reason than inadequate pollination, then bees must be brought in. Even so, honeybees are frail performers when a short blossoming season and rough weather run together, just when they are most wanted amongst the blossom. This is the time when bumble- · bees, which work in all weathers, are worth their weight in gold; their population can be encouraged by leaving some rough grass and banks for their nests and by discouraging mice.

Systems of Apple Growing.—The choice of rootstock depends on the system of apple growing adopted as well as on the acreage. The great majority of commercial orchards consist of vigorous bush trees relatively widely spaced, but various more intensive systems have been devised, particularly for small farms where the search for high production per acre is at its keenest. It is often claimed that intensive systems have the advantage in annual yield but this is not commonly proved in practice; 600 or more bushels an acre is a superb crop occasionally reached by both intensive and extensive orchards. What is true is that the intensive systems reach their maximum production more quickly. The various intensive and semi-intensive systems, English and Continental, are known according to the way the trees are formed and arranged, as dwarf pyramids, cordons, spindle bushes (*Spindelbusch*), pillars, and dwarf bushes.

Dwarf pyramids are stiff unstaked little trees on Type II or VII, with short branches bristling from a central stem stopped at about 8 ft. from the ground. They are planted in rows, usually 8 ft. apart with the trees 4 ft. apart in the rows — 1,361 trees to the acre; they begin to crop in their third year and can yield up to four tons an acre by their fifth. Dwarf pyramids are often recommended to newcomers but, in fact, far from being simple, the management of a really successful dwarf pyramid plantation is probably the most difficult job apple growing can offer, and generally pyramids go along at less than their best with an occasional brilliant season. The nicety of balance that has to be maintained is shown by the planting distance and the rootstock; Type II in freedom will grow to need 24 ft. square, pyramids are constricted throughout life to 8 × 4 ft. Restriction is obtained by grassing down, by the root competition between one tree and the next resulting from close planting, by controlled manuring and by the huge extra labour of summer pruning. The fact that the trees are restricted, checked, half-starved and kept so far from realizing their potentialities of growth is enough to disturb some people; it seems too unnatural to be right, and in practice growth is sometimes uncontrollably vigorous.

Cordons are an even more restricted form than pyramids, though at least dwarfing Type IX is used; there are no branches, but clusters of spurs along a single stem, which is kept tied at an ever decreasing angle to the ground to restrict the flow of sap. Cordons at 6 × 2 ft. take 3,630 trees to the acre and this, with the paraphernalia of wires, straining posts, canes, and the business of bending down and retying the cordons, as well as summer pruning, effectively counts out the system for present commercial use. Continental spindle bushes are also on Type IX; they re-resemble dwarf pyramids in being grown as a single vertical stem, but are allowed much more room. Fruit bud formation is brought about by bending down and individually tying the little side branches in summer, a process so fiddling that it is probably as bad as summer pruning if not worse.

Pillar trees – invented and named by the Berkshire grower Mr Gordon Maclean – are again trees of one central stem stopped at about 8 ft., with a bristle of perpetually renewed short side branches. Planting distance is 10 or 12 ft. × 5 or 6 ft. and Type II or even stronger stocks are used. Restriction is brought about by drastic winter pruning. A side branch grows out in its first year, forms fruit-buds in its second, blossoms and bears fruit in its third, and is then cut back to a stub which next spring throws a new strong shoot and the process starts again. A balance of first, second and third year shoots is maintained in each tree and regular crops of 300 bushels an acre are claimed. The system is experimental and the trees look dreadful with their chopped-off stubs and spray of shoots like the remains of a besom broom. It is really the renewal system of pruning (see p 92*ff*) carried to an extreme conclusion.

The last of these intensive and semi-intensive systems is the growing of dwarf bushes on Type IX, the trees dwarfed only by rootstock effect, allowed to grow as freely as they may and given all the room they need; an ordinary orchard scaled down by Type IX with its attendant advantages of easy spraying, thinning, picking and pruning, and its disadvantages of delicacy, weak anchorage and drooping habit. In order to yield crops as heavy as those of bigger trees that carry fruit bearing wood upwards, dwarf bushes have to be planted as closely as possible, which means that ordinary farm machinery cannot get through. The usual permanent distance of 12 ft. square takes 302 trees to the acre. The small scale machinery required is relatively cheap but of limited capacity so that the acreage that can be managed is strictly limited. A big acreage of closely planted

Type IX means several sets of small machines; the same acreage would be far more economically used by fewer, bigger trees widely spaced and served by one outfit of big capacity. Machinery cultivates or mows, spreads fertilisers, carts fruit, and sprays. It is the spraying that is critical as it has to be so closely timed, and although other mechanical operations can be spread out, the spraying machine should be able to get round in three or four days, and certainly in under a week. A run of bad weather can play havoc with the spraying programme if the machine is of inadequate capacity.

Filler Trees.—This matter of close planting introduces the use of filler trees, about which opinions vary. Trees planted on Type II at 24 ft. square (75 to the acre) obviously take many years to occupy the ground economically, so that it is usual to interplant with filler trees to make as full use as possible of the land from the beginning. A common arrangement is to plant a filler tree in the centre of each square, thus doubling the number of trees to the acre. Type IX has sometimes been used for the filler trees in such a plant of Type II, but it is not a good idea, with the trees mixed in size and the two rootstocks demanding different sorts of farming. Any block of trees, however mixed the varieties, is best grown on one uniform rootstock. Besides, if very lightly pruned, trees on Type II can be brought into cropping nearly as soon as on Type IX and the only differential treatment between permanent and filler trees is then the pruning. Or all the trees can be treated lightly at first and then more strictly as heavy cropping slows down growth. If Type IX trees are wanted to pay for themselves quickly and to finance further planting of more vigorous trees, slower to come to profit, they are best kept in a block by themselves. In the same way soft fruit for quick returns is much better kept on its own than under-planted in an apple orchard. The old fruit farm mixture of plums, apples, pears and cherries in one orchard, with currants and gooseberries below and strawberries between, would be a horror nowadays, impossible either to spray or cultivate; mixed II and IX is a minor example of the same thing. The trouble with a block of Type IX on a holding being developed with more vigorous trees is that the IX's continue to need their own small machinery, which soon becomes inadequate for the bigger trees; and then the bigger trees' machinery cannot get through the IX's. Even apples on two different planting systems thus do not mix well on one holding.

When the trees in a closely-planted orchard begin to crowd, out must come the fillers, either to the bonfire or to be transplanted. Transplanting such sizeable trees is a big undertaking, and the transplants become patients requiring a good two years' nursing — de-blossoming, watering, mulching and staking. Thinning is a terrible thing to have to do in a young orchard, and if the original plant has been too close the fillers must begin to come out just when they are nicely into heavy cropping; if thinning is delayed the shoots search upwards to the light and the fruit spurs are shaded out below; yields and quality suffer and spraying becomes more and more an impossible struggle in an orchard which has become a copse. 'Cutting up' – i.e. pruning back to let the sprayer through – only forces growth and crop more skyward. The fruitful tree spreads sideways, and is as broad as high. It is probably uneconomic to plant an orchard for more than one thinning, which, to make the fillers worth while, should not be necessary for some fifteen years.

The first few crops of a new plantation, particularly on Type IX, are often disappointing. The apples come over-large and coarsely finished – some varieties are worse than others – and are unusually subject to cracking, russeting and splitting, before the trees' root system has taken a deep and confident hold. A young apple tree, bearing precociously, is in an abnormal state; age settles it into normality and a balance of growth and cropping. If there is plenty of land and the grower can afford to wait for his crops, a wide plant from the start and no fillers is best; early crops are exchanged for a vigorous framework. A professional

man planting for support in retirement several years
ahead would be better suited thus than by a closer plant
of dwarfs requiring the maximum of attention right from
the beginning.

Before deciding whether or not to plant for quick returns
it is as well to know just what crops the different rootstocks are capable of producing in their early years. Fortunately a current rootstock trial at East Malling is available to give the answer. The trees in this trial are growing
in a good loam and their cropping has not been interfered
with by spring frosts. Pruning has purposely been extremely
light – lighter than in commercial practice – in order to
bring out as conspicuously as possible the differential
rootstock effects. The trees were planted in November
1945 and the latest report deals with their first five crops —
1948–52. On Type IX, Cox has carried a total crop in
the five years of 72 lb. per tree. Supposing that the trees had
been planted on a new farm in a block to themselves at
12 ft. square, their first seven years would have yielded,
at this rate, a total crop of 543 bushels to the acre. Supposing that the whole crop, all grades, averaged 30s a
bushel, which is optimistic, the gross return would have
been £815 per acre.

On Type II the Cox crop per tree was 111 lb. If these
trees had been planted as a new orchard at 24 ft. square
with one filler tree in the centre of each square (a total
of 150 trees to the acre, and they could hardly have been
put closer) the first seven years' yield would have been
416 bushels per acre, or by the same reckoning, £624. If
the trees had been on MM 104 (180 lb. per tree), at 150
to the acre the result would have been 675 bushels or
£1,012; on M IV (172 lb. per tree) at the same spacing,
645 bushels or £967; on M VII or MM 106 (identical
results, 145 lb. per tree) at, say, 20 ft. with the squares
middled, 218 trees to the acre, 790 bushels or £1,185.
The very vigorous new rootstock M XXV (140 lb. per
tree), even if planted at 30 ft. square, each square middled
with a filler on the same stock, would have yielded 336

bushels or £504. Transferring these individual tree results to acreage returns depends on a rather arbitrary choice of planting distance for each rootstock, and juggling with planting distances can largely alter results; M IX for instance could well be closer than 12 ft. square in a small plantation where only two-wheeled machinery is to be used

Enough has been said to show how closely choice of varieties, rootstocks and planting systems depend on the acreage to be planted; this cannot be overlaboured. My own choice, if I were limited to a maximum of 5 acres and was looking for the most economic return from the minimum capital, would be Fortune, Cox and Winston as dwarf bushes on Type IX — all three well suited to IX on good land and fully companionable for pollination. For a rather larger acreage I should compromise with a semi-dwarfing rootstock, VII or MM 106. For more than 10 acres I should have nothing to do with either dwarfs or big trees and should plant only on MM 104. At the moment my varieties would be chosen from Fortune, Merton Worcester, Cox and Bowden's Seedling.

Planting Plans.—When all these considerations of variety, rootstock and acreage, pollinators and fillers, have been well weighed, a new orchard can at last be planned on paper. The arrangement of the trees on the ground deserves more thought than it usually gets. The simpler the plan the better, as long as the trees have equal shares of space above and below the ground, and the tree rows are straight for tractor work. Only square, quincunx and rectangular arrangements need to be considered, though these can be complicated enough when planned to be thinned and yet retain the same distribution of pollinators. A square plant is self-explanatory; if a filler tree is planted in the centre of each square the arrangement becomes quincunx and the directions of cultivation become diagonals across the original squares, as Figure 1 shows. If a square design is started with, a first thinning, removing alternate diagonal rows, leaves a quincunx arrangement; a second thinning, removing alternate trees in every row along the opposite diagonal,

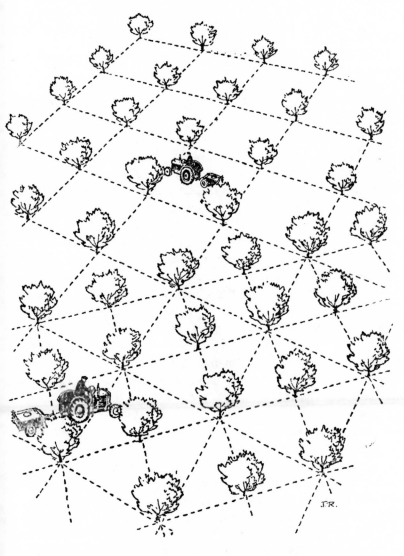

Figure 1. *Square and quincunx plants*

When a square plant (top) is interplanted with one tree in the centre
of each square the arrangement becomes quincunx (bottom) and the
tree rows become the diagonals of the original squares.

restores a square plant. The rows of permanent trees should be arranged to run as nearly north and south as possible.

In a mixed orchard the varieties are best arranged in rows for mutual pollination, two rows of Cox as it might be, then one or two of Fortune, two of Cox again, and so on. Each Cox is then always next door to a Fortune. This facilitates differential spraying and manurial treatments, and makes picking easier. But when, as in a block of Cox, any other variety is purely subsidiary and grown only as pollinator, a much greater proportion of the ground can be given to the main variety. The common arrangement is then the 'one in nine,' as called, when every fourth tree in every fourth row is a pollinator. One of the eight next door neighbours of every tree of the main variety is then a pollinator. This arrangement makes differential spraying and manuring much more awkward, as well as fruit picking on the isolated trees, and the chances of effective pollination may be dangerously slender. In fact the pollinator trees have sometimes been treated purely as blossom trees, with their fruitlets picked off in the summer to make sure of a show of blossom next spring. Such pollinators of course must blossom copiously and unfailingly, and exactly match the main variety in flowering season. Except for one variety orchards – usually Cox, Worcester or Bramley – the one in nine arrangement seems unnecessarily risky and over-specialized, unless the main variety is at least partly self-fertile. A one in four distribution of pollinators on a similar system, every other tree of alternate rows being a pollinator, provides for more effective pollination; but mixed orchards are certainly the safest of all, when two or three different varieties can be considered 'main.' The more varieties grown the less critical need be the matching of their flowering times.

Filler trees can be main or subsidiary varieties as required, though in mixed orchards it is as well to alternate the varieties of filler and permanent rows. In planning for one or two thinnings it is important to make sure that the right proportion and distribution of pollinators is preserved at each stage. Where each row is designed to be of only one variety, this arrangement cannot be maintained both before and after thinning, so the rows should be arranged to come right after thinning, when the greater part of the orchard's life is still to come.

The shortcoming of square and quincunx plants is that when they need to be thinned it is not because the trees are crowding each other, but because they are crowding the tractor. A more forward-looking arrangement, which avoids this difficulty, is the rectangular plant, as in dwarf pyramid plantations, where the trees in effect are grown as parallel hedges. Bush trees can be spaced in the rows two-thirds or three-quarters of the distance between the rows. Thus the rectangular counterpart of a 24 ft. square plant would be alleys 24 ft. wide, with the trees 16 or 18 ft. apart in the rows; 113 or 100 trees to the acre as against 75 in the square plant. Such a rectangular plant is the rational design for a future of the fullest possible mechanization, of automatic spraying and of offset cultivation machinery. There is, always room for the tractor to run up and down the alleys, and if a thinning is required it is solely because the trees are growing into each other. A rectangular plant is easily planned for thinning; an original plant of 21 × 14, for instance, is thinned by removing alternate trees in each row, leaving a plant 28 × 21 with the new alleys at right angles to the original direction. A block of Type IX trees would be more easily managed as, say, a 15 × 10 ft. permanent rectangular plant than as a 12 ft. square plant and would lose only 12 trees to the acre (290 against 302); or if planned for thinning, the plant could start at 8 × 12 ft. and finish at 16 × 12. A Type VII plant rearranged from 20 ft. square to 20 × 15 gains 36 trees to the acre (109 against 145), or, if the squares were going to be middled, loses 73 trees (218 against 145).

In tree numbers per acre a permanent rectangular plant from the beginning thus falls between the stages of a more orthodox quincunx beginning thinned to a square ending.

A rectangular plant, spaced for no thinning, thus gives
a reasonably good cover of the ground from the start and
the great convenience of having different varieties segre-
gated in separate rows lasts throughout the life of the
orchard. When continuous automatic spraying is used in
a square plant something like one-third of the wash is
directed into empty air; in a rectangular plant nearly all
of it reaches the hedgerow of trees. In the early years of a
rectangular planted orchard machinery can work both in
the alleys and across the tree rows, but later on the rows
become narrow uncultivatable strips where the ground
growth must either be occasionally cut by hand or kept
smothered by a continuous mulch.

The spacing and arrangement of the trees, the inclusion
or not of fillers, the mixing of varieties or a minimum
allowance of pollinators, can be argued indefinitely; it
depends largely on the worth and area of the land to be
planted. However, a rectangular plant does seem most
likely to suit orchard practice of the future; and it is convenient for the present.

Chapter Four

PLANTING AND EQUIPPING
AN ORCHARD

THE operations required to turn an empty field into an orchard are, first, fencing it against rabbits, then cultivating the soil into a suitable condition for planting, and then marking out the tree sites, planting the trees, staking, tying, spraying, pruning and manuring them. In comparison with the long debates and uncertainties of planning, action is simple and straightforward.

Pre-planting Work.—The wire-netting fencing needs to be of 1¼ in. mesh and 4½ ft. wide, the bottom 6 in. turned outwards and pegged down; there is no need to bury this apron and grass growing through soon locks it to the ground. 18-gauge netting is usual, although the heavier 16-gauge is well worth the considerable extra expense. The top of the netting can be fixed with netting fasteners to well-strained 8-gauge plain galvanized wire, and the fence finished off with a strand of barbed wire 6 in. higher. If the fence is to be cattle-proof two more facing strands of barbed wire are necessary lower down, or better still, the three strands of barbed wire erected as a separate fence 2 ft. outside the netting. If a boundary windbreak is necessary the sooner it goes in the better. Red-twigged lime, which makes a reasonably narrow and quick-growing tree, is popular at present. Lombardy is the only suitable poplar, though its roots are far spreading and greedy, and it is liable to harbour Silver Leaf fungus. *Cupressus macrocarpa* is the quickest of the evergreens but may be killed out in an exceptionally cold winter.

Autumn ploughing, with the furrows left rough to be broken down by frost, is the best preparation for planting. Trees can be successfully planted direct into an old pasture or ley, but only if it is in beautiful condition, full of white clover and smooth and level enough for close mowing;

even so, and for several years afterwards, the young trees will require protection from competition by the sward, by either hand hoeing or mulching. Unless it means destroying an exceptional sward, ploughing is the safest preparation, subsoiling at the same time if necessary; young trees get a splendid start in ploughed-in, rotted turf. The land is best worked down by cultivator, disc-harrow or rotary hoe, even before the tree sites are marked out, so that the field is level from the start. If soil analysis showed a low percentage of organic matter it is worth while sowing a bulky cover crop in late summer or early autumn for turning-in in the following spring. Any deficiencies of lime, phosphate or potash indicated by analysis are best made good by dressings broadcast before planting; analysis and recommendation for correction usually go together. This service is provided by the NAAS.

The trees should be ordered in good time from a first-rate nurseryman; there are not many of them and their order books may contain entries for two or more years ahead. The first expense of buying trees should be the last, and cheap lots, such as the poor bare-rooted trees found in auction markets, are the falsest of economies. The number of trees required per acre is obtained by multiplying together the two figures of the planting distance in feet and dividing the result into 43,560. Maiden (one-year-old) trees are generally used nowadays for planting-up new orchards, and now that nurserymen have realized that this is what is wanted the overpruned three- or four-year-old nursery specimens, looking like black currant bushes, are happily going out, though still insisted on by private gardeners. What nurserymen are wont to call 'extra heavy well-feathered maidens' are the trees to buy; they should be at least 4 ft. high with sufficient feathers, i.e. side shoots, high enough above the graft union to provide the first tier of primary branches. Strong roots are even more important; all the fibrous roots die on transplanting, it is the woody roots which count and they are often broken by careless lifting in the nursery. The rootstocks on which the trees are worked should have been taken from beds duly certified under the Ministry of Agriculture's scheme for ensuring truth to name and freedom from disease. Well grown maidens seem to have settled to a price of about £25 a hundred. Nurserymen who are also commercial growers and who take their bud and graft wood from fruiting trees are less likely to propagate virus diseases than those who must collect propagation wood from non-fruiting nursery rows. Some nurserymen claim that their trees are propagated from particularly fruitful 'strains'; this does no harm.

A heeling-in trench, a foot wide and a foot deep, rabbit proof, should be prepared for the bundles of trees. On arrival they are carefully laid over and temporarily planted in the trench. It is more convenient to give the trees their winter tar oil spray while they are still heeled-in, instead of chasing after them all over the field after they have been planted.

Marking out a field for planting is simply a matter of projecting a straight base line and erecting right angles from it. Cross staff and surveyor's chain are unnecessary; any sort of light chain, marked at intervals according to planting distances, is all that is needed for measuring over the ground and can also be used for laying off right angles in accordance with *Euclid*, Book I, 47 (In a triangle with sides proportionate in length to 30 : 40 : 50 the largest angle will be a right angle). Instead of a cross staff, which is an optical instrument for sighting right angles, a piece of plywood can be used: the plywood about 2 ft. square, with two lines at right angles drawn on it and marked by de-headed nails tacked in vertically, and mounted on a stake or on a camera tripod (see Figure 2). An old table small enough to carry about, with a line of nails close along two adjacent sides, is just as good. Light bamboo canes 3 or 4 ft. long are better than stakes for marking the tree positions. Set out a straight row of canes, planting a distance apart, along the longest side of the field; this is the base line. From each end of this line erect a right angle and mark these two further lines by canes at planting distance apart. Join their ends to complete a rectangle and mark this fourth line by canes at planting distance intervals. All the tree positions can now be filled in by sighting in two directions at right angles, either across or along the rectangle. It can be done single-handed, at the expense of a great

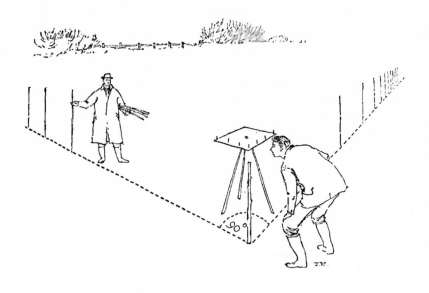

Figure 2. Marking out a right angle
Using a home-made sighting table, set up over a corner stake.

deal of walking to and fro; much quicker if there are two people to sight in two directions and a third to carry the bundle of canes and stick them in as directed by the boundary line spectators, as in Figure 3.

A quincunx plant is marked out on the square first, the squares afterwards 'middled' by sighting along the diagonals. On undulating or sloping ground longer stakes have to be used; ground measurement along sighted lines soon builds up errors. Where the tree rows are two or three hundred yards long, a few bigger and longer stakes painted black and white are necessary, and a pair of binoculars makes the work much easier; it is a job for a sunny day when the

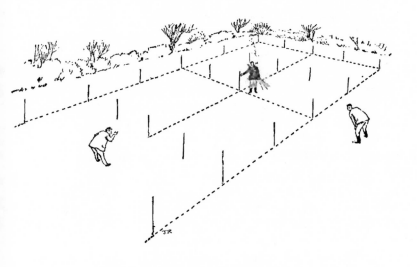

Figure 3. Marking out a field for planting

Once a rectangle has been set out, all the tree positions inside it can be fixed by sighting in two directions; and extensions from it made as necessary by sighting and measuring.

canes or stakes show up brightly. There is no need to allow for internal roads – a tractor has got to be able to get through anyway – but the headlands should be really generous, the distance from the fence to the nearest tree never being less than one and a half times the planting distance.

Tree Planting.—Planting can be done any time when the soil condition is suitable between leaf-fall and late March. Early spring planting has the advantage of having let frost get at the furrows; soil conditions may often be better, but the work is liable to end in a rush of cultivating, marking out and planting as the soil begins to dry out after the winter rains. Autumn planted trees probably suffer less of a check because new root growth in established trees often begins as early as January. But like so many agricultural operations, tree planting is often a matter of getting the job done at all rather than done at the exactly correct moment. If trees have to be mauled into heavy land in a late wet spring, it is worthwhile incorporating some old compost or even sand in the tree holes. The old rules about firm planting hold good: spread out the roots, work a nice tilth of soil among them and tread firmly — short jabs with a boot heel and the knee kept straight is the way. The graft union must be clear of the ground; if the union is buried the stem may strike its own roots – scion rooting, as called – and override the influence of the rootstock.

Maiden trees do not usually require a hole more than 18 in. across by 9 in. deep; the bottom of the hole should be broken up and left slightly mounded, and the sides should be straight, not basin-shaped. An ordinary fork and spade are satisfactory in ordinary soil, but for heavy or stony land navvying forks with steel sheathed handles are essential and admirably unbreakable tools. Most of the hard work of planting, at least of maiden trees, can be avoided by hiring or borrowing a tractor-driven post-hole borer with an 18-in. auger, otherwise it is all incurably manual labour. When the holes are dug by hand it is worth using a planting board to make sure of planting the tree in the exact position of the marking cane. A planting board is a piece of wood about 5 ft. long with a notch cut in each end, and another notch cut in the middle of one side. It is laid flat on the ground and positioned so that the marking cane comes in the middle notch; drive in a peg in each of the end notches, remove board and cane, and dig the hole. Then when the board is laid down again, spanning the hole and located by the two pegs, the middle notch indicates the exact position for the tree stem.

No manure should be buried at planting time unless a handful of bonemeal is scattered in the hole, a refinement some planters practise. After planting, a mulch round each tree of two or three forkfuls of dung generously covered with old straw is the best possible treatment and the only manure required for the first season. Half rotten straw or spoilt hay and a handful or two of dried blood can be used instead. Mulching is far better than the alternative of a patch of bare, hoed earth round each tree. Always keep the tree stems clear, or voles are likely to gnaw the bark under cover of the mulch; their damage is sometimes serious, even to old trees.

If there is time the stakes are best driven into the tree holes before planting. A single stout stake about 3 ft. long, 18 in. above and below ground, is all that is required for bush trees, unless on Type IX or IV, and should last until the tree can stand up on its own. The top of the stake should come just below the lowest branches and should be driven in vertically a few inches away from the tree stem, on its south-west side. Peeled chestnut is often used, but round section stakes grip the soil much less well than cleft or sawn stakes. Stakes are usually too flimsy and soon rot; they should really be half-length fence posts, well dried and well pickled in a timber preservative before use. Full-sized fence posts are best for trees on Types IX and IV, however disproportionate they may look at first. A tall stake soon turns out to be useful for Type IX trees, for when the branches are drooping with fruit they can be strung up with baler twine to a big nail driven into the top of the stake, making a maypole of it. Angle-iron or lengths of galvanized piping are excellent if heavy enough, but are generally too expensive; an iron stake should weigh 10 lb. to be effective as a permanency.

Various materials can be used for tying tree to stake: folded strips of sacking; salvaged or new baler twine, doubled or quadrupled; coir yarn — which is the light coconut fibre rope used for stringing hops; fancy plastic buckles; old rope, old rubber hose threaded with fencing wire, old bicycle tyres. The tyres are the best and should last two years without attention; inelastic materials need annual retying to prevent chafing or strangulation of the tree. The trouble with tyres, as with so many useful scrap materials, is to get enough of them. The wire rims are filletted off with a knife and lengths of tyre used as figure of eight ties — one end nailed to the stake, the other end passed round the tree stem, crossed over, with a round turn to stiffen it if necessary, and brought back to be nailed to the other side of the stake; use large-headed galvanized nails. Inner tubes are no use.

Some of the larger nurserymen undertake contract planting; they will mark out the field, supply and plant the trees, stake, tie, and prune them. This is worth consideration where an orchard is planned for retirement and the owner cannot spare the time for the heavy initial and non-recurring work of planting, or where trustworthy labour is not available. Another method of planting a field to apples, the cheapest of all but not so far mentioned because it is neither commercial nor professional practice, is that of planting out rootstocks and budding or grafting them a year later where they stand. There is thus no transplanting check and trees so raised soon catch up bought-in maidens planted at the same time. A recognizable and fruit-bearing tree can be produced in three seasons (or four if the season while the rootstock is establishing itself is included). Planting out rootstocks is of course very quick, hardly more than a spade slit being necessary, and their cost may be as little as one-tenth that of maiden trees. Many growers and nurserymen are ready to sell graftwood, which is no more than stout shoots of one-year-old wood saved at pruning time. Naturally it is necessary to be a competent hand at grafting or budding, but these are not difficult skills for any reasonably neat-fingered person to acquire. The ordinary whip and tongue graft is the method, and the best way to learn is to watch someone else doing it and then practise with any bits of hedge trimmings. If budding in July rather than grafting in March is done it is

wise to put two buds to each rootstock, then if both 'take'
to select the stronger when they begin to grow out in the
spring. In any case it is necessary to have a reserve nursery
row, worked at the same time, for replacing failures or
casualties. The grower can, of course, raise his own maidens
and plant them out in the ordinary way; this is less unortho-
dox and nearly achieves the same economy, but loses the
advantage of no transplanting.

Initial Pruning.—After planting, pruning. Except for
specialized forms like cordons or dwarf pyramids, trees
are described as standard, half-standard or bush according
to the length of clear stem; only bushes with a leg of from
18–30 in. need be considered. Commerical bush trees can
have three forms of head, natural habit, open centre and
delayed open centre. Natural habit means that the trees
are largely left to themselves. The difference between the
other two forms is only that the main branches of an open
centre bush are all a single year's crop of side shoots from
the main stem, which is then stopped, whereas the main
branches of a delayed open centre bush are taken from
the stem over a period of two or more growing seasons.
The result is that the primary branches of an open centre
bush all spring from perhaps 6 in. of stem, while the many
more primary branches of a delayed open centre bush are
spread over 2 or 3 or 4 ft. of stem; in both cases the main
stem is stopped by being cut back to the base of the highest
side branch. A delayed open centre head with the branches
taken over two or three seasons – over 2 or 3 ft. of stem –
is probably the most useful, though the stems of Type IX
bushes are best kept going until they reach the top of their
stakes, and any trees put out on a close rectangular design
are better suited for automatic spraying if formed rather
on the lines of dwarf pyramids than as short-legged and
spreading bushes. An open centre bush relies on three, four
or five primary branches, a delayed open centre on at
least double the number, so the loss of a branch by breakage
is less serious. But too many, too crowded branches are
worse than too few.

Where the desirable strong, feathered type of maiden has been planted and a delayed open centre bush is to be formed, all side shoots up to 18 in. from the ground are first cut off. The best of the remainder are selected as future primary branches, retaining only shoots which make a wide angle with the stem and are nicely disposed round it, not on top of each other; their tips should be at least a foot apart. The matter of wide-angled crotches is important because when the shoots have become branches those making a narrow angle with the stem are easily broken away with the weight of fruit, while wide-angled branches safely carry a heavy load. Shorten any side shoots over a foot in length back to a foot and leave any less than that untouched. Cut back the stem of the maiden tree to a bud about 9 in. above the highest feather; this bud should grow out strongly and continue the main stem. The bud next below it should be sliced off; if left it usually grows too vertically. The two or three buds below the topmost can generally be relied on to grow out, though rather less strongly, and they will make the next tier of branches above those produced by the feathers.

Some varieties do not readily make side shoots in their nursery year. The pruning of such unfeathered maidens, bare whips 3 or 4 ft. long, is similar: cut off the top to a bud 2 ft. or 30 in. above the ground and slice off the next bud. The next two or three buds downwards will make primary branches and further buds lower down the stem can be encouraged to break into growth and make more potential branches by the practice known as notching. This means cutting a shallow V sideways in the stem, through the bark and into the wood, immediately above a bud. Notch two buds on opposite sides of the stem a few inches below the top ones and not immediately in line below them. Some varieties answer better than others to notching and it is possible thus to produce all the necessary side branches without cutting back the main stem at all, though the stem is likely to be so whippy that it needs tying to a long cane. Notched buds usually produce broad-angled branches; as a general rule the farther the bud below the topmost, the wider angled branch it makes.

Early Management.—Once the little trees have been sprayed, planted, staked and tied, pruned and manured, the initial establishment is done once and for all. However insignificant the little sticks look, dotted across an expanse of brown earth, the field has become a young orchard; the future consists of management, while the trees perform their miracle of increase.

Orchard management is little trouble in the early years. Tree nutrition is looked after by the mulch of dung. Weeds are kept under control by infrequent cultivation, with hand hoeing round the trees if the soil is left bare. Common practice at present is to clean cultivate for the first five years and then to sow down the orchard to at any rate a potentially permanent sward. As long as mulching is practised to protect the young trees from grass competition there is every advantage in grassing down sooner, even as soon as planting is completed. This is dealt with later. Meanwhile clean cultivation is a misnomer; weed growth is welcome and necessary to slow down the loss of organic matter under arable conditions. Cultivation is only required to prevent perennial weeds becoming established and is usually stopped in late July, leaving the weeds to grow as they may until the following spring.

Spraying in the early years is simple enough; young trees usually grow vigorously and healthily, untroubled by many of the nuisances which are the target of later routine protective sprays; pests and diseases come with the fruit. If the maiden trees were sprayed with tar oil before planting, two lime sulphur sprays, one in mid-April with an insecticide added and the next at the end of April or early May, alone, should be all that is necessary for the rest of the season. If the trees were not sprayed before planting, or when fully dormant, a DNOC spray in mid-March will be necessary before the lime sulphur. Any blossom should be snipped off in the first season, whatever the age of the trees at planting.

Equipment and Costs.—Spraying and cultivation are the
two orchard operations done by machinery of one sort
or another right from the start; all else is hand-work at
first, though some jobs can be mechanized when the
orchard justifies it. Orchard sprayers cost from £10 to
£1,000, yet none can do more than wet the trees. The whole
of spraying is no more than wetting every part of the trees
and it is when the trees are big and dense that the physical
problem becomes formidable. It is solved by brute force,
using pumps working at up to a pressure of 600 lb. to the
square inch and turning out twenty or more gallons a
minute. Some spray damage which occurs is not of chemical
origin at all, but simply bruising of the leaves by the spray
blast. If time were unlimited, the lowliest form of knapsack
sprayer would do the job just as well as the leviathans
roaring in their own gale, but only if the nozzle could be
brought within 2 ft. of every part of the tree. The hydraulic
spraying of universal practice appears both wasteful and
inefficient. A large volume of water is used to dilute a
relatively tiny amount of chemical — 2 lb. of lead arsenate
for instance, or two gall. of lime sulphur, to 100 gall. of
water – simply in order to distribute the chemical evenly
over the trees. Much of the wash reaches the ground and is
wasted, and apparently much of the labour, time, fuel,
water cartage, pumping and mixing are wasted too. But
high volume hydraulic spraying, when well done, has
proved itself by safety and reliability; the trees cannot be
oversprayed because all but a film of wash runs off.

Active experiment is going on in what the Americans
call concentrate spraying, using either neat chemicals or
strong solutions atomised into mist in the way of a paint
gun and driven into the trees by air blast; air instead of
water is the diluent and the droplets of spray become
microscopically small; it is the difference between rain and
fog. Appropriate machines are already available in this
country, but there is little commercial experience of them.
Some aim to produce the same results with five or ten
gall. of wash per acre as that given by 300 or 400 gall.

of a high volume spray. The danger of concentrate spraying is overspraying, of loading the leaf with a phytotoxic amount of chemical; the safety run-off no longer operates when the chemical is laid on in a rapidly drying mist. Concentrate spraying also requires much calmer conditions. At present a compromise of a fairly strong wash at about fifty gall. an acre for mature trees seems to be the most likely development. Spraying machines are developing so fast that the most sensible course for a new planter is to make do with a small or secondhand orthodox machine in the expectation that medium or low volume sprayers will be proved in the next few years, by the time the original sprayer is due for replacement. Dry dusting is a useful but inessential summer auxiliary to wet spraying; hand worked rotary dusters are inexpensive, but dusting is unlikely ever to compete with wet spraying on tree fruits.

The old knapsack sprayer in its modern lightweight form with a detachable pump, costing from £10 to £20, will serve a new plantation for the first two or three seasons. Thereafter a larger capacity machine will be necessary, according to acreage and rootstock. Detachable spray pumps are available for many of the small two-wheel walking tractors, rotary hoes and motor scythes now on the market. The spray tank is either mounted on the machine or towed; a twenty-five-gallons tank is the limit for mounting, fifty gallons for towing. Next up the scale are detachable pumps for the small three or four-wheel ridden tractors, with towed or mounted tanks. But what have become the standard machines nowadays for fruit farms of ten acres or more are the specialized trailer sprayers, self-engined or driven by the power take-off of the towing tractor, with tank capacities from 60 to 400 gall., and costing from about £150 to £600. For automatic spraying they are fitted with a single or double bank of fixed nozzles at the back of the machine, for hand spraying they supply at least two lances. Portable headland pumps, using lances at the end of a great length of spray hose, or underground mains with a central pumping plant in the buildings, belong to the past.

The modern machine is mobile and self-contained, and although lance spraying is probably the most efficient way in good hands it is slow and expensive in labour, and can be expected gradually to go on giving way to the one-man outfit of tractor driver, tractor and trailer sprayer, trundling slowly along the tree alleys, with the fixed nozzles hissing unknowingly a travelling drench of spray into trees or empty air, like the rain from heaven that falls indifferently upon the just and the unjust. The most ambitious machines throw in a gale, provided by a sawn-off aeroplane propellor, and belong to ranches beyond any acreage envisaged in this book.

Hand lances are usually 2 to 4 ft. long with a single or double nozzle or a broom-head of three or more nozzles; modern grip or trigger taps make them easier to use. Using a short lance, hand spraying by the tractor driver from the tractor seat is a practical proposition in some orchards, particularly when the sprayer has its own separate engine. In America manufacturers have developed a swivel mounting for a spray gun on the tractor bonnet, but such ideas are hardly known in England; one-man farms are uncommon in England, common enough in America.

Spray nozzles are made up of a disc with a fixed hole and a swirl plate behind it, adjustable to control the width, coarseness and carrying power of the beam of spray. Discs are measured in $\frac{1}{64}$ in.; $\frac{3}{64}$ in, $\frac{4}{64}$ in. and $\frac{5}{64}$ in. being the most commonly used sizes. The old distinction of a fine misty spray for fungicides, where a fine film over leaf and fruit is wanted, and a coarse drenching spray for insecticides is now somewhat academic, as combined sprays are used whenever possible to avoid a separate round. But egg-killing winter washes should go on in a strong drench, to reach every tiny crevice of fruit spur and bark. Blockages and sticking valves are always with us; clean water should always be pumped through the sprayer at the end of the day and it is well to finish up with spindle oil

Cultivating and mowing machinery follows a similar scale to sprayers, except that there is no knapsack level;

scythes and hand-forks are non-starters nowadays. Ten acres or more of fruit demands a four-wheel or crawler tractor, a trailer sprayer and either towed or mounted cultivating and mowing machines. The modern tractor drawn and powered rotary hoe is probably the best orchard cultivator, though disc harrows are excellent and cannot tear up roots; spring-tooth harrows are effective on light land. The choice of grass cutting machines until recently was only between the ordinary reciprocating type of farm hay mower and gang mowers, but now the Hayter cutters offer a third method. These use square horizontal plates, with a single section of mower knife bolted to each corner, spinning at very high speed; they cut in the same way as one whips off a thistle head with a stick. The various models, self-engined or tractor powered, cut a swath of from 2 ft. with the smallest hand pushed machine to nearly 18 ft. when three gangs, each cutting 6 ft., are hooked up together behind a hard working tractor. Hayter cutters have the advantage over gang mowers in first cost (about £100 against £200 for a six-foot swath), are less easily damaged and much cheaper to maintain. Prunings up to half an inch in diameter can be left lying for the knives to slice up and scatter, and the machine can be used along the edge of a tree mulch, neatly undercutting the straw without disturbing it. Hayter cutters can be widely offset from the tractor and, being very low, can work under the branches and close up to the tree stems, but if given the chance will neatly shave off young trees at ground level. Gang mowers cut more closely and chop up and scatter the mowings better, but they cannot work so close to the trees and are not for stony ground. Reciprocating mowers cut hay well enough, but make a poor job of keeping a sward.

A new tractor, medium-sized trailer sprayer, grass cutter and cultivator will cost about £1,000, or about half this amount second-hand. Narrowed-down versions of farm tractors are made for orchard work — strictly for level ground.

At the two-wheeled walking end of the scale the choice

is among a motor-scythe with detachable spray pump, a rotary hoe with spray pump and cutter bar as accessories, or a market garden tractor with spray pump, cutter bar, and cultivator frame or rotary hoe as attachments. Here the first cost is about £120 for motor scythe and spray pump, or £150 for a small rotary cultivator with spraying and cutter bar attachments. A motor scythe and pump would serve a small grassed plantation of Type IX trees indefinitely and, if the initial cultivations and the sowing down soon after planting were done by contract, this would be the only machinery required. Three feet is the usual swath width for motor scythes and one at least will manage a four-foot bar, but all these machines using reciprocating knives suffer the same disadvantage as larger farm mowers; they cut tall stemmy grass well but are apt to push over rather than cut a short leafy sward and are fouled by the clip left lying from earlier cuts. Walking up and down all day behind these barking and shuddering machines is not to be commended; some at least can be alleviated by bogey seats. A front mounted cylinder mower attachment, cutting a 3-foot swath and costing about £30, is now available for later models of the Allen motor scythe; this may turn out to be the answer to the mowing problem in small scale orchards.

Small three- or four-wheeled ridden tractors fill the gap between the two-wheelers and full-scale farm tractors. Here also belong the small market garden crawler tractors, which have much in their favour. They are so small, low and narrow that they can get through a plantation where there is hardly walking room. Their power take-off will drive a high pressure trailer sprayer, they have enough speed to pull gang mowers, and they are unconcerned by steep land or loose soils.

Any orchard needs some sort of trailer – a sizeable car trailer will do on a small place – and for grassed orchards harrows and a roller are the only other implements needed from the start. A fertilizer distributor of the spinner type will probably be wanted later, but a bucket is all that

Plate I. (*Above*) A paddock cultivated and marked out at 8 × 12 feet for planting apples on Type IX. Using a planting board before the holes are dug (see page 70). (*Below, left*) A well feathered maiden apple pruned, staked and mulched (March). (*Right*) The season's growth (October). Tydeman's Late Orange on Type II.

is needed to begin with. The hand tools needed are digging, fencing and pruning tools. A knife is the best pruning tool for very young trees, and a pruning or grafting knife has a simple straight blade, sharpened to a chisel edge, not one of the fearsome scimitars often offered. Rolcut secateurs are the universal tools for older trees.

Buildings can be extremely modest at the start. Somewhere to keep machinery dry and to stack a few bushels of fruit is all that is wanted, and if there is nothing in existence a rough shed of straw bales and corrugated iron will do. More ambitious buildings, such as packing shed and store, can safely be left for several years.

The cost of establishing an orchard varies enormously. Small parcels of accommodation land suitable for apple planting are unlikely to be found for much less than £100 an acre. Complete farms are usually cheaper than this, particularly in the eastern counties, and present prices range from about £60 an acre upwards, including house and buildings.

Planting and equipping an orchard and maintaining it for the five or six years until fruit sales balance expenses costs from £150 to £300 an acre; this includes everything — machinery of sufficient scope to serve mature trees, as well as pre-planting expenses such as fencing, the usual annual expenses of fuel, manures, sprays, etc, and labour at the rate of one man to ten acres. Economies can be achieved chiefly on the handy-man, smallholder scale, where no outside labour is employed and picking and packing is a family affair. Raising one's own trees makes a very big saving, and lesser savings come from cutting one's own fencing and tree stakes. Collecting up spoilt stumps of hay, rick bottoms, wet straw bales, roadside mowings – being in fact a rag and bone man in search of humus – saves some bills, so does the manure from smallholders' pigs and poultry. Buying old machinery cheaply and doing it up saves much of the capital expense for those with the knowledge to do it and the patience to use it.

What profit may result from all the expense and waiting

F

of bringing a new orchard into bearing is wholly uncertain. All that can be said is to repeat the current average yields of well-managed, well-sited mature orchards – 250 to 300 bushels an acre and a profit of the order of £100 an acre – and to note that the grubbing of old orchards and the planting of new goes on as merrily as ever.

Chapter Five

ORCHARD MANAGEMENT

THE leaf is the tree's factory. If the leaf is right, dark green, strong and leathery in mid-summer, neither rank nor weak and pale, everything else will be right, at least as far as soil management and protective spraying are concerned. The leaf is the judge of good or bad management, and management carries its influence below ground by manuring, cultivation and cover cropping, and above ground by spraying and pruning. These are the main operations of annual maintenance, with always the leaf and summer growth as indicator, long before the crop itself gives the final verdict on season and grower.

The great object of soil management is to build up or at least maintain the soil's content of organic matter, which goes far beyond the mere supply of mineral nutrients needed annually for tree growth and cropping. The compost controversy, organic against inorganic fertilizers, is not what it was, now that the prime importance of humus is everywhere recognized; and in orchards a soil well loaded with bulky organic matter, steadily breaking down into humus and steadily renewed, is the greatest safeguard to tree growth and cropping and the best defence against variations in rainfall — whether too little or too much. The free and healthy growth given by humus-rich soils certainly helps fruit trees to resist the attack of pests and diseases, though the sweeping claims sometimes still made by the extreme left-wing of the compost party, that resistance can be complete and spraying unnecessary, are unfortunately not substantiated in commercial apple orchards. Spraying remains unwelcome but essential, expensive, unpleasant and sometimes ineffective.

Swards.—Any land summer-fallowed rapidly loses organic matter by oxidation, and in orchards the weed growth cultivated in is insufficient to keep up the level. The growing and turning-in of short term cover crops or the supply of bulky organic manures such as wool shoddy are essential, and expensive. The alternative is a grass sward, and every year more growers make the exchange of cultivator for mower; a tightly mown permanent sward is in fact fast becoming standard practice in modern apple orchards. Commercial practice has got riskily ahead of research in grassed orchards and the precise way in which a sward affects apple trees is not fully known. There is no agreement about the best types of grasses to sow, nor how short the grass should be cut. What is agreed is that the grass must be cut frequently and that the clippings must be left lying to rot down and to be pulled in by worms; the grass must be cut whenever it has made about 6 in. of growth and a hay crop never taken. Mowing is certainly no cheaper than clean cultivation; the machinery is more expensive both to buy and maintain and, though much quicker over the ground, ten or fifteen mowings in a season are needed as against three or four cultivations.

Whatever the means by which grass influences trees, the results are clear. Fruit colour is greatly improved, premature dropping of the fruit is largely prevented and its storage life is lengthened. Fruit size may suffer, because of the competition between grass and tree roots for available moisture and nutrients, and tree growth may be curtailed. Young orchards are apt to suffer a sharp set-back when put to grass and it takes several seasons before trees and grass settle down amicably together and the sward begins to show its benefits. Soil structure under grass is greatly improved, the organic content is safeguarded and slowly increased, and the worm population – the great indicator of fertility under English conditions – increases enormously. Orchard work all the year round is easier and more pleasant on a sward, particularly at harvest time, and in winter the grass roots give some bite for tractor traffic. The smooth greensward under the pattern of trees is always a joy to see, reinforced by the knowledge (or the hope) that it is secretly doing good.

At present about 10 lb. to the acre of rye grass or timothy and a pound or two of wild white clover is the common prescription for orchard sowing, complicated mixtures being thought unnecessary. The Aberystwyth extreme pasture strains – S23 rye grass and S50 timothy – are best, whichever grass is chosen. Both have their supporters. Timothy is dwarfer in growth, requires less mowing, and probably competes less with the trees; it is the advisory officer's favourite at the moment, but there has simply not been enough or long enough research so far for reliable indication of the best grass mixtures, let alone their optimum management under varying conditions. Analysis of the changes in composition of sown swards over a period of years, under differing mowing and manurial treatments on various soils, and the varying effect on trees, is a huge subject for investigation, so far hardly touched.

Chewing's fescue has sometimes been used, particularly on dry gravelly soils, for it lies like hair and hardly needs mowing. But it does not persist well and in any case grass is not simply an inert thatch but a lively builder of fertility, its increment of leaf perpetually being cut and sent back to feed first the teeming soil fauna and flora and then the tree roots. But exuberant cocksfoot, at the opposite extreme from the fescues, and the quickest builder of fibre below ground, is too strong for orchard use. Some growers are happy to sow only clovers and to let natural grasses come in on their own, as they soon will. Any soil, fallowed or derelict, falls down to grass in a season or two if nothing at all is done except mowing; on some soils the little weed grass, *Poa annua*, is at first the only grass to show, but its quick cover is by no means to be despised.

Clovers are nearly always included in orchard seed mixtures because of their faculty of nitrogen fixation; atmospheric nitrogen fixed by the root nodules of a good sward of wild white clover can in one season amount to the equivalent of 10 cwt. of sulphate of ammonia per acre, but probably only a small proportion of this ever reaches the tree roots. Whenever any sward is cut a proportionate amount of roots die, and in the case of legumes this means that nitrogen in the root nodules, fixed by bacteria for the plant's own use, is released to the soil; the more a clover crop is cut the more nitrogen is released, and in arable farming, for instance, a preparatory crop of red clover cut three times shows a better yield in a following potato crop than if cut only twice. Yet recent research has questioned the value of clovers in orchard swards; leaf analysis shows a better match between grass and apple foliage than between clover and apple, and mown clover may release nitrogen late in the season when it is not wanted. Clovers usually do not persist well under orchard conditions, dying out in shade and under heavy dressings of inorganic nitrogen. Even so I am sure the aim in sowing down a young orchard should be to produce a clovery sward and to keep it as long as possible; my own fancy is to sow clovers only and to let the grasses come as they will. The sowing rate of clovers alone needs to be rather heavier than when included in a grass mixture. Wild white clover, of which S184 is the best strain, is the most persistent of all clovers and should be the basis of a long term sward, though I like to add some S100 white clover for quick cover and bulk. The biennial American sweet clover (*Melilotus alba*) and the annual yellow trefoil or hop clover (*Medicago lupulina*), with their far-seeking nitrogen-fixing roots and their rapid bulk of herbage, are splendid fertility builders, and on rundown land make a good start for a more permanent sward. Seed of both is relatively cheap; a sowing of two or three pounds to the acre of each and a pound each of S184 and S100 white clovers is my own idea of starting an orchard sward. Alternatively the sweet and hop clovers can be sown alone, and one or two seasons later heavily harrowed and oversown with white clovers.

Herbs are sometimes included for their deep root tillage and their efficiency in mineral extraction, but their value in orchards is at present theoretical — they *ought* to be useful. Chicory is the likeliest, with its tremendous tap root and its copious leafage; it persists for a few seasons under

close mowing but gradually loses vigour; it belongs naturally to calcareous clays and will not 'take' on some soils,
but where it will I think five pounds an acre worth including
with the clovers. When the roots eventually die they must
leave deep cores in the soil, improving aeration and drainage, as well as leaving a good organic residue. Dandelions
perform the same function and can be relied on to find their
own way to an orchard; even docks would not be unwelcome if it were not for their harbouring of a troublesome
insect, the dock sawfly, whose little green caterpillars leave
the docks in late summer, climb the trees in search of winter
quarters and bore holes in the apples.

Clover seed can be broadcast by hand at low rates if it
is mixed with many times its volume of dry sand, but using
a seed fiddle is easier. Analysis may show the need for a
preparatory winter dressing of phosphates – basic slag
or superphosphate – and possibly of lime if the soil is
markedly acid. Sowing can be in spring or late summer;
summer sowings are less of a check to the trees. Harrow,
broadcast, harrow again and roll, and the job is done.

Once a sward is established vigorous harrowing every
early spring is essential, leaving as much brown earth
showing as green grass. The roller traditionally follows, to
firm the roots, but I suspect its only real use is to consoli-
date the surface for mowing and to squash in loose stones;
then close mowing from the time there is anything to cut
until the branches droop too low with the crop. Some
growers like to leave a bulk of herbage to stand through
the winter and carry traffic, others give a final trim after
harvest, even in November, keeping the worms busy and
discouraging field mice.

Current practice, as already mentioned, is to keep a
newly planted orchard under clean cultivation for the first
five years and then to grass down, though the fashion for
earlier grassing is spreading, and there seems every reason
for it; why spend five years burning up the organic content
of largely vacant soil when fertility could be slowly building
under clover and grass? In any case the immediate area

round the trees requires hand work, either hoeing or mulching. I have found no reason to alter my own practice of sowing down immediately after planting or later in the same season, but the young trees require continuous heavy mulching for several years.

Mulching.—Where the chief danger of clean cultivation is loss of organic matter, with swards the danger is of starving and droughting the trees with grass, of trying to grow two crops in soil with moisture for only one. Mulching is the great cure-all in either system. A mulch round the trees works in several ways: mechanically, by largely suppressing competitive weed growth, by acting as a one way filter, keeping the soil moist and cool yet letting through rainfall and, biologically, by slowly rotting down and releasing humus and nutrients to the soil, like woodland leaf litter. The sideways movement of soil moisture is fairly free when the soil is wet but becomes increasingly restricted as the soil dries, so that moisture under a mulch is hardly drawn off sideways however bone-dry the surrounding soil; a good mulch can save for the trees at least a month's rainfall, which would otherwise be lost in evaporation by wind and sun.

Almost any organic material which will rot, or is rotting, can be used for mulching. Spoilt hay is best of all, especially if it has heated enough to kill the grass seeds, but the choice is usually confined to baled straw as being the only material available in sufficient quantity and easily handled. Needless to say wet bales should not be bought by weight, or much money will be spent on water; dry bales usually go between twenty-five and thirty to the ton and wet ones are best bought by number on that calculation. Four young trees will get a good cover from each bale, and the wetter and more rotten the straw the better. There is a slight fire danger with dry straw which also is apt to blow away until it has weathered and worms have locked it to the soil. Any initial mulch, particularly if dry, must go on while the soil is still moist or the material will absorb more rainfall than it lets through. On some hot gravelly soils, as in Essex, where rainfall is too low to grow both trees and grass and the need for humus most pressing, most of the orchard surface is kept strawed.

There is one important precaution to observe when mulching with organic materials like straw, or even more so with sawdust, which are nearly all cellulose and very deficient in nitrogen. The organisms which break down such material also require nitrogen and if it is not available in the material itself they take it from the soil; it is eventually returned, but meanwhile fresh straw laid on bare soil can produce a sharp nitrogen deficiency very quickly. Sawdust is worst of all and if laid thickly, fresh and dry, round a tree, can bring growth to a standstill by the nitrogen deficiency induced and by absorption of all the summer rainfall. So where fresh unrotted materials are used a proportionate amount of nitrogen must be added to feed the organisms; dried blood for those who stick out for organic manures, sulphate of ammonia or nitro-chalk for those who do not; ½ cwt. of 15 per cent nitrogen for every ton of straw. Straw bales are best stacked in low heaps for one or two seasons before use, so that they partly rot down. Sawdust is best heaped and wetted with all the water it will take, and layered with sulphate of ammonia at 1 cwt. to the ton, with 1 cwt. of chalk added to prevent acidity developing and stopping bacterial action; it should not be used until it is dark brown and half way to a mould, when it makes an excellent soil-improving mulch. Sawdust is still a waste material at some sawmills and can be bought for from 10s. to a £1 a ton; baled straw costs £3 or more a ton delivered nowadays. They mix well to make a long lasting mulch. Macerated bark from match factories is the latest mulch material, but too expensive for orchard use; in America tractor driven chipping machines are used to turn any sort of brushwood into mulch material.

All these mulches have to be brought in from outside the orchard, but where the trees are widely planted it may be possible to make an orchard self-supporting in mulches by letting the grass along the alleys grow up to hay height once or even twice in the season, then cutting it with an ordinary hay mower and shifting the unmade hay into the tree rows. Heavy doses of nitrogen would be necessary to get a good flush of grass and lucerne or red clover might well be a better proposition. The method has hardly been tried as yet but seems attractive, particularly for new, widely-planted orchards, even if close overall mowing is substituted later on when the trees, apart from leaving no room for haymaking, cast a useful shade of their own.

Manuring.—There are no hard and fast rules about the manuring of apples; tree performance is the only guide. As with other crops, high yields and high quality commonly go together, though with dessert apples particularly a level of nitrogenous manuring that will produce maximum yield adversely affects quality. Nitrogen, however, sometimes produces less effect than expected; in such cases lack of soil moisture or organic matter is probably the limiting factor to growth and cropping. On really deep moist soils relatively tiny fertilizer dressings are required. As a yardstick, an annual average extension growth of some 18 in. is about right for bearing trees; anything over 30 in. is getting too vigorous, or under one foot, too weak.

Now that most fertilizers are applied in inorganic form, nitrogen and potash are the only nutrients generally given as an annual routine, supported less regularly by phosphates and possibly lime for the sake of the sward. Phosphate deficiency has never been seen in orchards nor have phosphate dressings produced any recognizable effects in growth or cropping; some growers hold that phosphates make for harder, better-keeping apples, but this awaits experimental confirmation. The nitrogen needs of mature apple orchards are usually met with annual winter dressings of from 2 to 10 cwt. an acre of sulphate of ammonia, nitro chalk or nitrate of soda, and 1 to 2 cwt. of sulphate of potash (rather than muriate of potash), costing £5 to £10 an acre. Young orchards are most economically treated on a tree by tree basis, so many handfuls to each tree, until the roots come to occupy most of the ground, when overall dressings with a distributor or spinner are necessary. Five cwt. an acre –

an average nitrogen dressing for dessert apples in grass – is near enough 2 oz. a square yard. Nitrogen requirements are highest in grass, lowest in arable, and though the ideal of making an orchard self-supporting in nitrogen by means of clover is seldom if ever realized, a clovery sward certainly reduces the amount of 'bag' nitrogen required. Grass gradually reduces the requirements of potash, as the grass clippings continually left lying release soluble potash.

The NPK trio is undeniably the basis of plant nutrition, but over the years such crudely simplified fertilizing leads to unbalance in both soil and tree. Magnesium deficiency is the fashionable complaint at present, thought to be brought on by overdoing potash, as potash and magnesium are supposed to be antagonistic — though many orchards never show magnesium deficiency even after years of heavy potash dressings. As a soil dressing magnesium sulphate (commercial Epsom salts) is slow and expensive, and essential in the long run, though foliage sprays (20 lb. of the salt to 100 galls of water) applied several times during the growing season, and compatible with most fungicides and insecticides, usually temporarily remove the symptoms. Magnesium deficiency needs to be taken seriously, for untreated trees soon become poor and unthrifty. Magnesium is the only deficiency commonly treated by foliage sprays, though the American technique of spraying urea (5 lb. to 100 gall.) to get nitrogen quickly into the trees is being tried by some growers.

The various symptoms of mineral deficiencies are a matter for advisory officers in the first place, but once identified are easily recognized again. Nitrogen deficiency with its shiny reddened bark, small pale leaves and small brilliant fruit, and potash deficiency with its marginal leaf scorch – the leaves looking as though they had been singed – are the commonest. Magnesium deficiency is often characterized by a peculiarly selective premature leaf fall, so that in late summer the new shoots show bare except for a tuft of leaves at the tip; and the leaves are purpled or browned before they drop. Deficiencies of trace elements are more often due to their being in unavailable form rather than actually missing from the soil; a new technique in compounding trace elements – producing the so-called sequestrenes – may make correction by soil dressings effective, when direct applications as simple salts are at once locked up. Sequestrene iron, manganese, zinc, copper, aluminium and magnesium are available, and very expensive.

Grassing down and organic manuring go a long way towards maintaining a safe balance and preventing deficiencies; organic manures are undoubtedly safer than inorganic, far more expensive, and much longer lasting. The scarcity of dung has made its value rather an academic matter nowadays, though it is often considered to produce too rank a growth in dessert apples, unless on poor soils; various slaughterhouse wastes – concentrated like dried blood, meat and bone, hoof and horn; or bulky, like wool shoddy, feathers and rabbit fur – are the substitutes. Probably the merit of organic manures and composts is in the unknowns and unidentifieds — trace elements in available form, vitamins and hormones. The sensible course seems to be to mix inorganic, for cheapness and convenience, with organic, for safety, long effect and for the unknowns, and to grass down and mulch for soil structure and humus. And if tree growth, crops and fruit size are still inadequate in a dry year the only course left is orchard irrigation. The expense makes it a matter for last resort; an eventual decision to irrigate does not affect the initial planning of a new plantation.

Pruning.—No such saving of labour and expense as inorganic fertilizers give over bulky organics can be contrived in the large and essential work of pruning; it remains handwork in winter weather and the only consolation is that the season for it, from leaf-fall to the end of March, is nearly six months long. However, the modern methods of regulated or renewal pruning do involve a lot less cutting than older systems of close spur pruning. Advisory officers have been taught renewal pruning – it is the official system nowadays – and the obvious way to learn it is to see it done, by attending or asking for a demonstration. It is hardly possible to learn pruning from the written word, unless the reader is already used to cutting trees, but something must be said about the reasons for pruning. A totally unpruned tree crops first of all, but soon becomes a thicket; it loses vigour, the crops become irregular and the fruit comes small and poorly coloured from the shade. Spray penetration is impeded and the restriction of free air movement makes the foliage slow to dry after rain, encouraging the infection and spread of fungus diseases. Pruning encourages growth, reduces cropping and increases fruit size; the more a tree is cut the more it is stimulated into growth and the less it fruits. The great object of pruning is to keep the trees open to air and sun and, working in with manuring, to maintain a balance of growth and fruit. While the fruitlets swell in summer, next year's fruit-buds are forming, and wood is growing for the buds of the year after that; and while it all goes on the trees must be open and airy enough for a bird to fly through.

Just as the types of tree head – natural habit, delayed open centre and open centre – rise in ascending order from least to most formative cutting, so the three common maintenance pruning systems – regulated, renewal and established-spur – range from least to most annual cutting. Regulated pruning and natural habit heads go together and make the nearest commercial approach to no pruning at all; virtually the only cutting done is the removal of crossing, rubbing or much overcrowded branches and shoots. Regulating pruning is appropriate for bringing filler trees into early bearing and for big cookers where detailed work is impossible. The crop is spread over all the sources of fruit bud, springing direct from two-year-old wood (and even one-year-old in some varieties), from new spurs on the three-year-old, and from established, branched spurs on older wood. Fruit buds on young wood flower later than on spurs, so blossom time is spread out. Strict spur-pruning is at the opposite extreme; the whole crop is carried on established spurs and most of the increment of new wood is cut away every year. Spur-pruning goes naturally with funnel-shaped open centre bushes and properly belongs to trees and soils of less than moderate vigour, where both hard pruning and heavy manuring are needed to keep the trees going. The straight branches clustered with spurs look neat and well cared-for but produce neither the best coloured apples nor the heaviest crops, though the apples are the biggest. The spur systems branch and increase and, unless kept thinned out, become like little forests of coral.

Renewal pruning, developed particularly by Mr C. R. Thompson, author of *The Pruning of Apples and Pears by Renewal Methods*, 1949, and by Mr W. C. Kent, the SE provincial fruit specialist of the NAAS, is less strict. Like regulated pruning, it aims at spreading the crop over both young wood and old spurs, but also at renewal, at keeping up a perpetual fount of fruiting growth. Grow, fruit, cut back and grow again is the cycle, and free-growing trees can thus be kept at an optimum size and in a nice balance of growth and crop. Leading shoots are treated similarly in renewal and established-spur pruning; the systems differ chiefly in their treatment of laterals. (The leader is the shoot extending the tip of a branch; laterals are the side shoots.) Established-spur laterals are cut back progressively to produce artificial spurs originating from fruit buds; in renewal pruning some laterals are left uncut to make fruit buds, some are shortened to keep up the supply of new laterals, and some older wood is cut back each year to stimulate strong shoots which will grow into replacement branches. In both cases the leaders are treated similarly, tipped or left uncut according to the vigour of the trees. Once the main branches have been selected in a young tree, some leader tipping is necessary to keep the tree shapely and vigorous. Cut to a bud pointing in the right direction, leaving from three-quarters to half the new growth. This also encourages laterals to grow out and prevents long bare areas from developing on the branches. Leaders growing too uprightly or too vigorously can either be pulled down and tied outwards for a season, after which they stay put, or cut back to a suitable lateral, turning that into a leader. There is little more to forming a young tree than this. Some growers leave the leaders untipped after three years, others tip at least some until they get out of reach. In order to give room for the laterals, particularly in renewal pruning, the ends of leaders – cut back or not– need to be at least a foot apart when the primary branches are selected, and always 2 ft. apart at any later stage. It is all very well to prune lightly at first, but as the branches come down with early cropping it is necessary to cut harder, going back towards the centre of the tree to encourage new shoots to come forward and replace the drooping ends of the original lowest branches. Brief, rule-of-thumb instructions for renewal pruning are given in an appendix.

Spraying.—As the pruning season ends so spraying begins, for the bulk of routine spraying is concentrated between mid-March and the end of June. The array of pests and diseases that attack apple trees vary enormously among varieties, orchards and districts, and from season to season. Routine spraying, which is essentially preventive, changes too, struggling to keep up. A new grower has a good summarized guide in East Malling's *Spray Calendar* (last edn 1949), though this is getting rather out of date, and the bigger spray chemical manufacturers produce first rate advisory booklets, revised every year, giving full instructions for the use of their sprays and other information besides. Cautionary notes on varietal susceptibilities and on the compatibility of various sprays need to be most carefully observed. Illustrations of the various stages of growth, and their accepted names, at which sprays are applied are given in the Ministry of Agriculture's Bulletin No. 137, *Fruit Bud Development*, and in most of the spraying guides. These stages, the life history of a fruit-bud, are 'dormant,' 'swelling,' 'breaking,' 'burst,' 'mouse-ear,' 'green cluster,' 'pink bud' (full bloom), '80 per cent petal-fall,' and two to three weeks later, 'fruitlet.' It may be noted that pest control is almost entirely a matter of killing the pests on the trees with poison sprays; research into biological control is virtually non-existent.

Poison spraying is complicated and restricted by the hope of sparing the friend while killing the foe. Sparing pollinating insects by avoiding insecticide spraying during blossom time is elementary, but cause and effect are usually less simple. Unwise use of DDT, for instance, can bring about a damaging build-up of red spider by killing insect predators like black-kneed capsids which prey on the mites. Stomach poisons, such as arsenate of lead, are automatically selective since they cannot kill until pests are caught in the act of nibbling leaf or fruit. Contact poisons like DDT cannot be selective in this way and in fact predators are often more susceptible than pests.

The chief pests and diseases and their topically appropriate drenches may be followed through the season. What can still be called a standard spraying programme consists of a late winter wash, chiefly for aphis, followed by two fungicide sprays before blossom, for scab, with an insecticide added to one or both for caterpillar; after, or even during, blossom at least two more weaker fungicides go on, either combined with or separate from a petal-fall insecticide or apple sawfly and another, later, for codling moth; a minimum of five or six separate sprays.

Tar oil when the buds are dormant (up to February) or DNOC as the buds burst (mid-March) are the standard winter egg-killing sprays. Both control aphis and apple sucker at the appropriate concentrations, and DNOC gives a partial control of winter moth caterpillars and of apple capsid. A year's progress in a young orchard can be lost if either aphides, which stunt and distort the shoots, or caterpillars, which can practically defoliate the trees, are allowed to romp uncontrolled. DNOC also kills most of the winter eggs of red spider, which, where they are thick, look like splashes of red paint on the bark. Red spider in fact is in some of the drier fruit growing districts the major apple orchard pest of the post-war era. The trees are seriously debilitated and their leaves bronzed by the

Plate III. (*Above*) Orchard mowing with the Hayter grass cutter.

(*Left*) Winston ready for picking in early November, the branches nearly leafless; a five year old tree on Type II.

Plate IV. (*Left*). A bush apple in a garden orchard after cleft grafting; three branches left as "sap drawers". (*Above*) The first season's growth from a 25 year old standard apple,

sap-sucking of hundreds of thousands of mites in late summer; fruit colour and finish is ruined, size reduced, and next year's fruit bud weakened. Variations on the standard spray programme in any orchard depend largely on whether or not red spider is a major problem. Winter washing is sometimes replaced for economy by one or two bud burst, mouse-ear or green cluster sprays of long persistent DDT emulsion or of BHC, or both, but the results have not been altogether successful and red spider is not controlled. DDT alone at bud burst or added to DNOC has put an end to the formerly troublesome apple-blossom weevil.

Scab is the subject of the next spray and lime sulphur is the usual protective, preventing the development of spring-released spores which rain washes on to the young leaves. Natural varietal resistance to scab is of great value, but may be transient, as in Bramley, and in any case susceptibility varies from area to area and the virulence of attack depends entirely on the season; warmth and wet make scab weather. Natural resistance to scab unfortunately does not imply a general resistance to fungus diseases. Some varieties resistant to scab, such as Jonathan and/or Bowden's Seedling, are unduly susceptible to powdery mildew; this mostly affects the tips of young shoots and is thus encouraged by modern methods of lighter pruning and untipped leaders. Sulphur sprays usually keep it in check, though cutting off and burning the pale infected shoots in winter and the mealy, distorted leaf rosettes in spring is a necessary support. Mildew is often associated with bad growing conditions — droughty shallow soils, lack of humus, and mineral deficiencies.

Two lime sulphur sprays before blossom, at green cluster and at pink bud, are a minimum number, and $2\frac{1}{2}$ per cent and 2 per cent dilution respectively is as much as – often more than – the trees will stand. Lime sulphur is long proven, effective and relatively cheap but the trees hate it; the yellowed and scorched leaves after spring spraying are sufficient sign, but effects last even to harvest, for a full lime sulphur programme undoubtedly affects fruit size, increases russeting, and is liable to cause leaf and fruit drop. The trees also hate lime sulphur's chief alternative, the various organic formulations of mercury salts. The two fungicides act differently, mercury being an eradicant which is not persistent but which can dry up existing scab infections, lime sulphur being a persistent protective but ineffective against existing infection. Lime sulphur used through spring and at 1 per cent in summer also often keeps red spider down to an undamaging level, but this may be less important now that new red spider ovicides (PCPBS and CPCBS) are available for summer spraying; in any case lime sulphur at 1 per cent is often unsafe after blossom. It is the lime in lime sulphur which causes scorch and 'hardens the leaf'; milder forms of elementary sulphur, without lime – colloidal and wettable or dispersible – are generally less effective and more expensive, though safer. New fungicides keep coming forward, but recent materials, if safe, have generally been found less effective than lime sulphur, or if as effective, then unsafe; they are also more expensive. A formulation of captan (SR406) is the latest and far the most promising, though extraordinarily expensive; it is said that until captan has been used right through the season no grower can be aware of the damage he has been doing with lime sulphur. Apart from expense, which may be recoverable by the heavier and better finished crops resulting from a captan programme, its use is likely to be restricted by the fact that it does not control mildew. Mildew is increasing and looks like becoming a major nuisance; sulphur remains the only effective check at present. After scab and mildew, the third troublesome fungus disease of apples, brown rot of the fruit, is unaffected by present fungicides, except that summer sprays of mercury do definitely reduce its incidence.

Lead arsenate or DDT is added to the green cluster fungicide to control caterpillars, and nicotine or BHC to a post-blossom fungicide to control apple sawfly, a damaging pest in some districts and absent in others. Another fungicide and a mid-June lead arsenate spray for codling moth caterpillars complete the minimum programme, but there cannot be many growers of high grade dessert apples who still get away with so few. It is not so much a matter of adding different sprays as of repeating the same ones more often, so that a film of poison awaits pest or disease from bud burst to within a few weeks of harvest. The cost of spray chemicals is small in young orchards, but as it rises so do yields; there can be few mature orchards now costing less than £15 an acre in spray materials. A brief spraying guide is given in an appendix.

Fruit Thinning.—The end of spraying sees the beginning of fruit thinning, for although the thinning of blossom or fruitlets by hormone spraying will no doubt come (from America as usual) it is at present too uncertain. Thinning remains old-fashioned hand-work, snipping off fruitlets with scissors or twisting them off with finger and thumb. It can start as soon as the inexplicable 'June drop' – which often extends into July – is over and shows what is left. Prevention of June drop, the opposite of thinning, may come to be yet another field of control for hormone spraying, but not yet.

The leaf as ever is the guide to thinning, and the stronger, darker and thicker it is the larger the crop that can be left. Varieties vary much in their need for thinning, some, such as Cox, Lambourne and Superb, seldom being thinned at all, and others, such as Epicure, Fortune, Miller's Seedling and, most of all, Winston, sometimes needing hard treatment. Long stalked apples can be left two to a cluster but short stalked varieties have to be thinned to singles, or usually one or the other will be pushed off as the fruit swell. The 'king apple,' the centre fruitlet of a cluster and usually the biggest and best, should always be removed as it is apt to develop into an apple over-large and mis-shapen, with a bossy stalk and defective storage qualities. Where very drastic thinning is necessary the trees have to be gone over more than once, for few growers can bear to be drastic enough in one operation. The thinnings lie and shrivel in the sun, the remainder swell towards harvest.

Chapter Six

THE APPLE HARVEST:
FRUIT QUALITY AND MARKETING

On a hundred acres of orchard and on one acre each apple is individually handled several times. Even in America apples are picked by hand, though no doubt some fearful suction picking machine is in development, with a blower at the delivery end to screen off the leaves, branches, birds, etc, inadvertently gathered with the fruit.

Picking.—Normal practice is to pick into buckets or bags slung across the shoulder and then to transfer the fruit into orchard boxes for transport to the buildings for grading and packing or for storage. Imported egg crates make useful orchard boxes for a small place, and are cheap, but many growers simply use 'salesman's empties,' when the fruit is to be marketed in them; small trees can be picked direct into boxes. A neat new technique is to use the half-bushel veneer boxes now available, carried on a simple sling. The same box serves in turn as picking-bucket, storage tray and non-returnable market container. Handling and thus bruising is minimized and the storage boxes are automatically renewed each season, instead of having to be cleaned and sterilized as with a permanent stock.

In commercial orchards the trees often have to be picked clear at one sweep, starting before and ending after the optimum time for each variety; the old rule that an apple is ready to pick when it parts from the spur on being lifted is the first to go by the board. Naturally it is best to work over the trees several times, starting as soon as a proportion of the fruit is ready, but the proving of pre-harvest hormone sprays, which delay the abscission of fruit stalk from spur, has certainly lessened the need. ANA – alpha-napthalene acetic acid – applied at ten parts per million a week or two before the fruit usually begins to drop, is effective on many varieties; much windfall loss is avoided and the fruit stays on the tree to reach its full maturity, size and colour. Pre-harvest hormone spraying has become an essential part of the culture of Beauty of Bath, so liable to premature dropping, is very useful with second early varieties like Worcester and Fortune, and is sometimes effective on late varieties like Cox. Very late varieties like Winston, Late Orange, Granny Smith and Wagener hang well on their own and must be left as long as possible if they are to develop their best dessert quality.

Bird damage is sometimes a major problem for which there is no final solution; shooting, scaring and perhaps trapping are all that can be done. Getting rid of birdpecked, or otherwise damaged, diseased or undersized fruit is not a marketing problem; it is best dropped on the ground as soon as picked. This is usually the only grading there is time for during picking, though some growers do manage to pick and grade as one operation, leaving only sizing to be done as the fruit is packed.

Packing.—Growing a good clean crop of apples is only a beginning, unless the grower is a member of a co-operative packing station, and exchanges freedom from all the work and worry of grading and packing, storage and marketing, for loss of the control of his own product. Many are only too glad to, as soon as the opportunity is offered. The market potentialities of an apple crop are realized only if a deal of trouble is taken over its presentation. The difference in the price made by a bushel of very best apples jumbled into a salesman's box and by exactly similar apples wrapped and packed in a non-returnable container is far too great to be ignored. The consumer can do no more to an apple than eat it, and apples are sold loose; it seems ridiculous that their value should be increased by putting a piece of paper round each one, but it is so and has to be accepted.

Apples are sold by weight in the shops, but by weight or number in the wholesale markets. The unit is a bushel which is 40 lb. of apples, but a stated number of apples of a certain size, and weighing within a pound or two of 40 lb., is also a bushel. Most of the English apple crop still goes to market in salesman's returnable bushel or half-bushel boxes, which are well enough for the lower grades, but are slowly being replaced by non-returnable packs for better quality fruit. Salesman's empties should always be lined; the cheap paper known as Blue Royal Hand is generally used and is available ready cut to line the sides and bottoms of standard bushel and half-bushel boxes. The boxes vary in weight so have to be weighed before as well as after packing. A label, a lid of paper or cardboard stapled on, and away they go.

Non-returnable packs – bushel, half-bushel and single layer trays – are made of wood or veneer or fibreboard and cost up to half a crown each for a bushel box, as against the sixpenny hire charge for a salesman's empty. Best dessert apples are often sold in half-boxes as they are supposed to yield the best return this way, even allowing for the extra cost of two boxes instead of one. Only the best grades of the best varieties are worth such packing and must be supported by close sizing and by wrapping. A small grower has against him all the weight of the closely standardized output of factory-like packhouses. His relatively little sendings must be as distinguished as can be contrived; fancy trimmings and neatly turned rolls of tissue paper are worth the trouble – always so long as the fruit is up to it.

There is, however, an entirely new method of apple packing, which can – or may – put even a one-man grower on the same basis as a big packhouse. This is the Hartmann apple tray pack, first developed in America, and using for apples a modification of the system fully established for egg packing. Soft fibre leaves, moulded to fit the cheek of an apple, are simply layered into a container, bushel and half-bushel boxes in either wood or fibreboard being available. The leaves are impregnated with mineral oil to keep the apples fresh and with differently moulded leaves, a full range of counts from 234 (2–2¼ in.) to 56 (3½–3¾ in.) apples to the bushel can be packed. The number of leaves required to make up a bushel pack varies according to size of apple from six to four, the top layer being covered with a further leaf upside down. When using these trays it is worth bedding the top layer of apples on a sheet of coloured tissue to improve the appearance. Blue tissue is usual, but green or yellow is sometimes used; green particularly is supposed to make apples look riper than they are. There is no wrapping and packing becomes unskilled. On a very small scale it may even be possible to pick and grade, size by eye, and pack in one operation beside the trees, but picking is usually far too urgent for such delaying tactics. These tray packs are hardly proved as yet, but so far have consistently made better money than apples packed in salesman's empties. Single layer trays, which only the best Cox is worthy to fill, are also made.

Another method of packing apples, already accepted and spreading fast in America, but hardly tried in this country, is pre-packaging on the farm; the apples are weighed off and sealed in the transparent plastic bags in which they are later sold in the shops; the bags are marketed loose in both returnable and non-returnable boxes.

The label on the end of a box of apples should state the variety and grade, count and/or size, and weight. Variety and grade go together as far as packing is concerned, non-returnable and returnable packs being used for both cookers and desserts, except that the half-bushel boxes, and, in a much smaller way, the single layer trays, are used only for dessert apples. The range in Bramleys, for instance, descends from wrapped apples in non-returnable boxes, to wrapped apples in returnables, to a jumble pack – i.e. the apples tipped in loose – in returnables. Grades are unlikely to be statutory again, as there is no demand among growers for the return of a National Mark; many, however, pack to the Ministry of Agriculture's recommended grades, published as *Marketing Leaflet No.* 101. These grades, so unfortunately reminiscent of back street stationery and sweet shops, are 'Extra Fancy,' 'Fancy' and 'Domestic,' with different standards for cooking and dessert varieties; the old National Mark's 'Super' grade has been dropped.

Extra Fancy dessert apples are over $2\frac{1}{4}$ in. in diameter,
free from blemish and of good colour and shape, with the
apples in any one container closely uniform in size and
colour. Fancy grade desserts are allowed a total area of
skin blemish of $\frac{3}{8}$ square inch, minumum size is reduced to
2 in., colour to 'normal,' and uniformity of colour and size
in any pack to 'reasonable.' Domestic grade desserts are
also over 2 in. in diameter, total blemish may be up to
$\frac{5}{8}$ square inch, and there are no requirements about colour
or uniformity of size. Cooking apples are allowed a larger
area of blemish, $\frac{3}{4}$ and $\frac{1}{2}$ square inch respectively for Domestic
and Fancy grades, with a minimum diameter of $2\frac{1}{4}$ in.;
Extra Fancy cookers must be over $2\frac{1}{2}$ in. The apples of all
three grades, dessert or cookers, must be 'clean, bright and in
good condition' and must have 'reached that stage of maturity
which allows the subsequent completion of the ripening
process'; all three grades must be 'free from such blemishes
and injuries as are calculated to impair keeping quality.'

The importance of colour is shown by that little difference
between 'good' (Extra Fancy) and 'normal' (Fancy). A box
of green Cox, however perfect in finish, size and shape,
can never be better than Fancy grade. Colour, of course,
comes from the orchard and not the packhouse, but many
late-keeping varieties, dull at picking, do brighten up
remarkably in the darkness of store. Colour is largely
unpredictable, as it varies so much from season to season
and from soil to soil. Grassed orchards give better colour
than arable, low nitrogen status better than high, and regulated or renewal pruned trees usually give brighter fruit
than spur pruned, partly owing to its better exposure.

Some growers include Extra Fancy with Fancy and call
the result Fancy Plus. The description of windfalls is a
matter of some nicety, for an apple is ineligible for a grade
name when even slightly bruised, though it may be
otherwise perfect; 'Selected Windfalls' is perhaps the best,
and Cox probably the only variety worth sending at all,
and then only if it can be got away in a hurry. A
September gale soon clutters up the markets.

Size is of great importance and in the orchard primarily depends on depth of soil and soil moisture. Dessert apples of the accepted commercial varieties are seldom too big except from young trees or when they come as a very light crop. The struggle is more often to get them big enough, by all or any of the effective means — hard pruning, drastic thinning, mulching, manuring with bulky organics, and irrigation. Colour is the first casualty in the struggle for size, so the result is always a compromise.

Yield and size are closely connected; a thousand apples between 2 and $2\frac{1}{8}$ in. in diameter make $2 \cdot 73$ bushels (American figures), while a thousand apples between $2\frac{3}{4}$ and $2\frac{7}{8}$ in. make $6 \cdot 21$ bushels. Apples are always measured in diameter; under 2 in. is unsaleable, or should be; $2-2\frac{1}{4}$ in. are 'smalls,' 234 to the bushel; $2\frac{1}{4}-2\frac{3}{4}$ in. covers the range of best commercial dessert, with the optimum size narrowly on either side of $2\frac{1}{2}$ in. and packing 175 to the bushel. The best size for cookers is between 3 and $3\frac{1}{2}$ in. Grading machines – which are only sizing machines, for all grading for quality is by eye – cost from about £70 upwards. A home-made sizing board does well enough to start with, a board drilled with a series of holes increasing in diameter by $\frac{1}{4}$ in. steps from a 2 in. beginning. It soon becomes easy to judge size to a quarter inch limit by eye, with only an occasional apple having to be offered to the board for test. Mechanical graders of course work more closely, but a spread of less than $\frac{3}{16}$ in. for any one count is unnecessary except in special cases.

The NAAS is interested in assisting the better presentation as well as the better growing of fruit, and from time to time arranges demonstrations of apple packing in the fruit growing counties. Written descriptions of standard methods of packing always make the job seem more complicated than it is; obviously the best way to learn how a professional finish is given to a box of apples is to attend a demonstration. Count and size in a half-bushel or bushel pack of apples are inseparable, except by tighter or looser packing, since the size of the box is fixed; the variables are the number of layers and the number of apples in a layer. Since a row of apples of one size seldom exactly fits the width of the box, the rows are staggered, with either the same number of apples in each row or one more or less. The pack starts across the near end of the box, a British standard bushel box, the box end on to the packer, ready lined with flat or corrugated paper and slightly tilted towards him. The apples are wrapped so that the folds of tissue make a protective pad; they are packed lying on their cheeks, stalk end away from the packer; a 9-in. square of tissue wraps a 2½-in. apple. The number of apples that will fit across the near end of the box decides the pack. If three will fit but not four, the pack will be 2–2, i.e. two apples to each row across the box. If four apples will fit but not five, the pack will be 3–2; if five but not six, 3–3. Merely these three packs cover a range of count and size in a British standard bushel box from 56 3½-in. apples in four layers to 213 2¼-in. apples in five layers.

Figure 4 shows how the packs are started. A 2–2 pack starts with the first apple in the left-hand corner of the box, and the second half way along to the right-hand corner. The two apples of the next row nest in the gaps between those of the first row, so that apple number four touches the right-hand side of the box; and so on, subsequent rows staggered to left or right until they reach the far end of the box. The next layer is the same but starts at the right-hand corner of the box and the apples ride in the pockets left between the apples of the first layer; and so on, until four layers have filled the box. The other packs are similar in that the apples of one row never touch each other. A 3–2 begins with a first row of three equally spaced apples, the two outside ones touching either side of the box; the next row of two apples nests in the gaps left, and so on; the second layer begins with a two. A 3–3 pack is staggered first one side then the other, like a 2–2 pack. The first row starts at the left-hand side of the box, with a gap between apple number three and the right-hand side. This gap is filled by the third apple of the next row, which touches the right-hand side of the box. The niceties of getting a tight finish at the far end of the box, and of arranging a bulge in the middle of the top layer, when a wooden lid is to be nailed on, are matters for demonstration. Fibreboard boxes are less demanding than wooden.

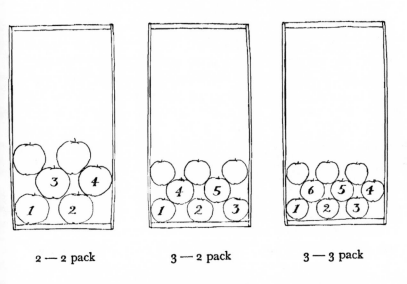

2 — 2 pack   3 — 2 pack   3 — 3 pack

Figure 4. Apple packs
How the three commonest apple packs are started, using non-returnable British standard bushel boxes. The apples must be wrapped.

Storage.—Apple storage means barn store to smaller growers, and so it will for the first several years of a new plantation on any scale. Cold or refrigerated gas stores, so essential for larger growers, are not justified by less than ten acres of late-keeping dessert apples in full bearing. A cold store is simply a very well insulated chamber with the temperature held at a uniform level, usually about 37°F;

a single chamber store is not likely to cost less than £1,500. Refrigerated gas stores are air-tight as well, and the fractions of oxygen and carbon dioxide in their atmospheres are maintained in a proportion appropriate to the apple variety being stored; the requirements of different varieties vary, thus, one chamber, one variety. The apples use up oxygen and give off carbon dioxide, the right proportions of which are regulated by controlled ventilation and by the chemical absorption of excess carbon dioxide.

The object of storing apples is simply to delay their ripening for as long as possible, and this depends very largely on temperature; a difference of even one or two degrees in the average storage temperature is reflected in storage life. A low steady temperature but protection from frost, a moist but not stagnant atmosphere, and at any rate partial darkness, are the conditions that a natural store has to fulfil as well as possible. A cellar is usually best of all, but many sorts of buildings will serve – barns, stables, outhouses – and the thicker the walls and roof the better. If part of the building is below ground so much the better, and if any excavation is being done – such as making use of a natural pit or digging into the side of a steep bank – the excavated earth can be heaped against the overground walls. An earth floor is as good as anything as long as it drains freely, and thick thatch the best roof. The least suitable stores are dry lofts and timber and corrugated iron sheds, where temperature varies wildly; lining such sheds with straw bales greatly improves matters but makes protection from rats and mice by small mesh wire netting more than ever necessary. A natural store should be kept as cool as possible by opening the doors whenever the air is cooler outside, as at night, and the apples should have lost as much as possible of their field heat before storing, by being left for a night under the stars and going into store first thing in the morning. Apples can be stored in any sort of box holding up to a bushel or so, and stacked in tiers; the veneer half-bushel boxes mentioned earlier are excellent as they contain little bulk of wood to draw moisture from

che fruit. Early and late apples should not be stored together because the effluvia from the early hastens the development of the late. Any sort of wrapping, even newspaper,
prolongs storage life; aluminium foil seems to be particularly effective, and thin plastic film is being tried; oiled
paper wraps are essential for gas storage. Apples taint
easily, so anything like paraffin or paint should be kept
well away.

The variations in storage behaviour within any apple
variety are made in the orchard. There is naturally much
uncontrollable seasonal variation, but storage life is closely
affected by cultural practice; apples keep better from
grassed orchards than from arable, and from heavy soils
than from light. A heavy crop stores better than a light
crop, and small apples better than large; the large fruits
from young trees are seldom fit for storing. A low nitrogen
status makes for better keeping qualities than a high, and
fruit from lightly pruned trees generally stores better than
from hard pruned. Apples picked slightly immature keep
longest, but tend to shrivel and never reach the quality
achieved by later gathered fruit.

Marketing.—The great bulk of English apples is sold by
commission salesmen in the fruit and vegetable markets
of the big towns. The fruit is out of the grower's control as
soon as it leaves the farm, and little more need be said except
that the salesman's commission – usually about 10 per cent
– is generally held to be reasonable and the retailer's
margin often excessive, or infamous. Local outlets are often
very useful to smaller growers, particularly for the early
crops from a new orchard. A grower selling direct to a
retail shop should get from two-thirds to three-quarters
of the selling price. Fruit thus sold can either be strictly
sized and graded, or sent less profitably, as 'orchard run' —
i.e. straight from the trees, with no more grading than the
throwing out of damaged and undersized fruit.

All sorts of ways of selling apples are open to individual
investigation – roadside sales, direct sales to institutions,
postal sales – and inexpensive advertising in local papers

can be helpful. Any fruit farm is something of an experimental station and there is just as much room for experiment in the storing, packing and selling of apples as there is in the growing of them.

Chapter Seven

A FEW OLD TREES

THE hundreds of acres of old commercial plantations, no longer economic, do not make the problem of a few old trees in a farm or home orchard any less acute to their owner. The solution to a large acreage is simple: pull out the trees with tractor and winch, particularly now that a government grant of up to half the cost is payable. This may often be the best way on a smaller scale too; the soil of old orchards is often highly fertile and could be better used if the trees were out of the way. If a few trees have any value for amenity or as shade trees and rubbing posts for stock they are better left alone, and any idea of producing commercial fruit from them firmly given up. This applies particularly to old farm orchards with forest-sized trees of apples and pears, plums and cherries all mixed up together.

Apart from leaving them alone or grubbing, what can be done with neglected trees depends on their condition, age and variety. Martyrdom to canker is often the lot of such trees, a fungus disease so far barely mentioned, as it should be little problem in new plantings on suitable sites. Canker cannot be cured by spraying though regular fungicide spraying to prevent scab also prevents the scab lesions in the bark by which canker can enter. Proprietary canker dressings can be tried, or the cankers cut out and the wounds painted over, but pruning back to clean wood is safest, when practicable. The rank growth induced by overdoing nitrogen is always more liable to canker infection than hard whalebone-like wood, and ill-drained heavy soils commonly favour canker. Flat-headed trees which have ceased to grow at the top and which throw a forest of 'water shoots' from old wood in the middle, usually indicate bad drainage; and the tree roots may make drainage

schemes impracticable. When such trees are badly can-
kered as well there is nothing for them but grubbing and
burning, a decision likely enough to be reinforced by the
site being low lying and liable to spring frost. Varietal
reaction to canker varies widely, Bramley and Worcester
being respectively the classic examples of considerable
resistance and undue susceptibility.

Old age in trees is more remediable than in their owners.
The drastic pruning known as dehorning, i.e. cutting
branches back to within a few feet of their origin, often
reinvigorates an aged tree, and a whole new head can be
formed. The work should be spread over several seasons,
dehorning a branch or two at a time. All renovation
pruning is work for a saw, fiddling little snippings with
secateurs being quite inappropriate. Saw cuts should be
made sloping so that rain is shed; the cuts should be pared
smooth round the edges with a knife or chisel, and the whole
surface given a protective coat of paint or a bitumen preparation. Dehorning is also the treatment for trees that have
grown too tall. This is often the result of overcrowding —
bare wood below and a tangle of branches reaching for the
light above; in such cases thinning must come first and
probably at least half the number of trees will have to
come out.

Even when its condition and age puts an apple orchard
within range of reclamation, there is still the vital matter of
variety. The commonest condition is the worst from the
commercial point of view — a perfect museum of different
varieties and only a tree or two of each; thus commercial
orchards began two or three centuries ago and thus home
and paddock plantings have continued ever since. Attempts
at local sales, backed by heroic home consumption, is the
usual harvest; the unsuitable shelves in the unsuitable fruit
store are laden in the autumn, and rotting fruit is gradually
picked out until there is nothing left; a frosty spring comes
as a blessing. All the same, condemnation need not be
wholesale; many good quality old varieties, like the Russets,
and some varieties of local repute, may be worth saving.

Any accepted commercial variety, even if no longer planted, is probably worth its place; there is little danger of clean fruit of varieties like Ribston Pippin and Blenheim Orange being unwanted, at any rate by local markets. Least hopeful are the numerous, mediocre, outmoded, early and mid-season cookers, and the euphemistically called dual purpose varieties, which are often neither. The first step is to get the trees identified, which may be a matter for an expert. The range of variation in the fruits of one variety grown under various conditions can be far greater than the difference between 'typical' specimens of distinct varieties, and experts may fail to agree. Old varieties no longer raised by nurserymen can also be baffling. An apple does need a name to be sold under, and if all else fails and the unknown variety seems a good one, an invented name is better than none. It may even prove to be justified, for stray seedlings crop up often enough and most of the two thousand or so varieties of apples now known were originally brought into cultivation as wildings from the woods and hedges. Marketing relatively small lots of apples from an orchard of mixed varieties is likely to need nearly as much effort as reclaiming the trees; it probably means discovering or even creating local or specialized outlets.

The ambitious solution for trees in reasonable condition but of out-dated or unsatisfactory varieties is to graft them over to something more suitable. The trees can either be topworked, i.e. completely reheaded, the main branches cut back to stumps and cleft grafted, or they can be frameworked, i.e. the original framework of the tree is retained but is refurnished with a great number of scions, put on as stub grafts or inserted in the bark by one or other of the methods of bark grafting. Topworked trees may take five years to bring the new variety into full bearing, by which time they will be good-sized trees again. Even so they never catch up frameworked trees in either size or cropping. Treated so much less drastically, frameworked trees begin to bear some fruit in the second season after grafting and are soon back into full cropping. However, in many cases full scale frameworking is simply not practicable; one, two or even three hundred scions may be needed to refurnish a big tree, as against a dozen at most for topworking. Thirty years is probably about the age limit for successful grafting. Cleft grafting is practicable for limbs up to 4 or 5 in. in diameter, but cuts larger than this may never fully heal over. Topworking is sometimes much interfered with by the same Silver Leaf Fungus so troublesome on plums, and with particularly susceptible varieties like Newton Wonder it is often impossible to prevent infection of the large wounds; any topworked orchard generally shows some Silver Leaf casualties. Like dehorning, grafting over old trees aims to bring at least some of the fruit back to within reach of the ground. This is not likely to happen if one has to get up a ladder before branches of less than 5 in. diameter can be found.

Cleft grafting is quick and simple, and has given a new lease of life to many an old tree. It is certainly the easiest way of dealing with trees with suitably sized branches near the ground. It is always better to cut back and graft only half the branches in a season, but if the tree is done all at once then some small branches must be left as 'sap-drawers,' to be cut off in the winter after grafting when they will have served their purpose. The grafting season begins in late February and can be carried safely into May. The trees can be prepared in winter by cutting back the branches, but not all the way; they have to be cut back again to give a fresh surface at grafting time. The scions, stout healthy shoots of one season's growth, are saved at pruning time or bought in if necessary. They usually keep well enough, dormant but fresh, when heeled into moist soil in a shady place but any that do show shrivelled bark or discoloured wood must be thrown out. The grafting itself is soon learnt; as usual the way to learn is to see it done. Small branches will take one or two scions, larger ones will take three or four in oblique clefts; avoid splitting the branch right across if possible. Eventual growth is generally needed from only one scion in each limb but the more that are put in to start with the quicker the wound heals.

The lower end of the scion is cut on either side of a bud – the 'graft bud' – to a long, equal-sided wedge, the cuts slightly inclined inwards so that the inner end of the wedge is narrower than the outer; the scions should be three to five buds long, cut off close above the topmost bud. A broad chisel can be used for striking the cleft, and a narrower one for prising it open to insert the scion, but a special clefting tool made up by a blacksmith is better. An old file can be used for this, first softened and then beaten out at the end to a knife edge like a meat chopper; and if the tang is sharpened it serves to open the cleft. With the cleft levered open, the scion is inserted so that the top of the wedge cut comes level with the sawn-off stock and the cambium layers of stock and scion – the inside edges of the bark – are nicely in contact. The cleft springs shut as the tool is removed and firmly pinches the scion; no other fastening is necessary. Figure 5 shows how all this is done.

For sealing over the cut surfaces after grafting bitumen emulsion is much more convenient than the usual hot waxes; plug open clefts with clay before sealing over. Shoots that break forth from the old wood have to be kept rubbed off and the new grafts need to be watched for damage by caterpillars and bark-eating weevils; DDT or lead arsenate are the cures. Tying some of the whippy vigorous young growths to canes secured to the old branches may be necessary during the first summer. Pruning thereafter should be as little as possible, no more than is required to guide, build-up and keep open the new head; bending and tying the new branches into position is better than cutting and promotes the formation of fruit buds. Growth from surplus scions is progressively removed as it crowds, cutting back to the graft union.

The choice of varieties for grafting an old orchard is just as difficult as for planting a new one, though less may be at stake. Not Bramley because of its increasing suscepti-bility to scab and because nothing can prevent its making a big tree, becoming more and more difficult to spray,

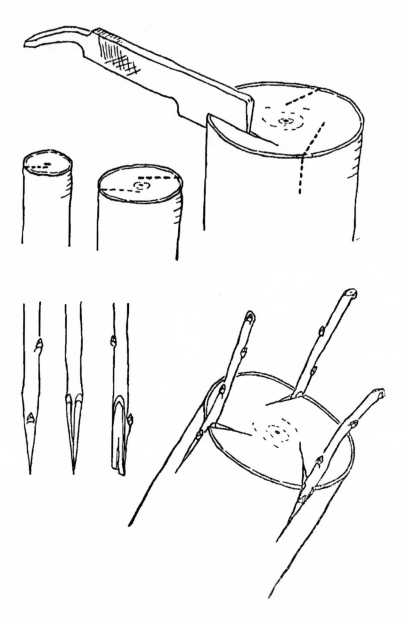

Figure 5. *Oblique cleft grafting*

and not Cox because of the detailed and painstaking cultivation it demands; certainly not Winston, because of the
problems of size and thinning. It is unreasonable to expect
to grow commercial apples without some spraying, but it is
sensible to choose varieties that will do with as little as
possible; a natural resistance to scab is the essential quality.
Arthur Turner, Grenadier, Edward VII and Lane's Prince
Albert have it among cookers; Edward VII seems the
likeliest choice, but its late flowering season makes it
difficult to find a suitable pollination companion. Among
commercial dessert apples Jonathan and Wagener are
nearly scab-proof, though both are liable to mildew.
Fortune seems to vary according to district from resistance
(excellent, in my experience) to susceptibility, and Lambourne seems to be the same, generally agreed to be resistant but in my particular experience, rather susceptible.
The Russets are usually free of scab and so are Charles
Ross, Miller's Seedling, Belle de Boskoop and D'Arcy
Spice. Beauty of Bath, Epicure, Ellison's Orange and Rival
usually show some resistance; Worcester, Blenheim, James
Grieve, Superb and Newton Wonder are the most susceptible of well-known varieties. In terms of spraying, a firm
scab resistance means clean fruit with no sulphur spraying
at all, a moderate resistance clean fruit with two pre-
blossom sprays only, except in a very scabby year.

Apart from grafting, renovation of a neglected orchard
means no more than renewing the ordinary annual maintenance in intensified form. After vigorous pruning, opening
up the trees to light and air, cutting out all the dead wood
and partly dehorning if necessary, an extra strong tar oil
spray will give a good clean up. Scraping off old loose bark
with a piece of wood before spraying is helpful. Extra
spraying at extra strength will probably be needed for a
season or two. Grass is the obvious soil management.
Existing grass may need no more than vigorous harrowing,
a dressing of phosphate, and regular mowing, but a tangle
of undergrowth on humpy ground is the more usual state,
requiring ploughing or rotary hoeing, working the land

down level and either re-seeding or allowing tumbledown grass to come. Manuring depends on the growth the trees are making; big cooking apples in a grazed orchard may need no nitrogen, a starved block of bush trees, red of bark and hardly growing, asks for a lot. It is doubtful whether stock-keeping is practicable in orchards expected to produce commercial crops. Trees big enough to be out of the way of cattle are unlikely to produce a good commercial sample and spraying will probably have to be by contract. Pigs make a fearful mess and manure the ground very unevenly; poultry and trees go well together but not poultry and spraying; regular spraying virtually closes a commercial orchard to all livestock from mid-March to the end of June. The idea of geese as self-supporting, self-propelled mowers is attractive, but unfortunately they are very vulnerable to poisoning by lead arsenate and DDT deposited on the grass, and, at any rate in young orchards, they soon start destroying trees by nibbling the bark.

It is evident that much thought has to be taken before deciding whether to reclaim or grub a neglected orchard. It should be one or the other because continued attempts to sell rubbishy fruit from neglected trees merely depresses the reputation of home-grown apples. Every old tree that comes out by the roots helps the fruit growing industry.

Chapter Eight

A YEAR'S WORK

At the turn of the year pruning is practically finished in some orchards, hardly begun in others. Nearly three months remain if pruning is to be finished before DNOC spraying begins, little more than a month before the buds begin to move and put a stop to tar oil spraying. The winter is never long enough, the days so short and the weather often unfit for outdoor work. Carting and spreading mulches and organic manures round the trees can fill week after week, but is best done either in late autumn before the land is winter wet, or in hard frost. Whatever job a tractor is doing it has to follow practically the same track up and down the alleys, and heavily laden wheels are bound to cause damaging soil compaction on wet ground; ruts can easily be cultivated out in an arable orchard, but once cut in a sward stay for good. In orchards through the winter the less seen of tractors the better.

Big prunings from saw cuts must be carted away and burnt, smaller snippings can be left lying; any graftwood wanted is saved at pruning time, bundled and labelled, and heeled-in in a shady place. Stakes and ties must be looked to for chafing or constriction; re-staking needs moist soil and bare trees — another job to be fitted into short winter days. Replacement stakes usually have to be driven at an angle of 45°, passing the stem; the head of the tree prevents the driving of another vertical stake like that used at planting time. Sowing inorganic fertilizers is the least of winter jobs, on a small scale a bucket and wheelbarrow job for any quiet dry day. Potash is better held in the soil than nitrogen and can go on any time in the winter, though there is no experimental evidence for choice between autumn, winter or spring for nitrogen application; February is the usual time, or January and March when a heavy dressing is split into two applications.

Hedging, ditching, drainage schemes and new planting can add to the press of outdoor work. If there is any doubt about orchard fences a walk round after a fresh snowfall is the time to see if any rabbits are getting in. In bad weather, winter indoor work is preparing tree stakes, fencing posts and ties, overhauling machinery, repairing or making up orchard or market boxes. An acreage of very late-keeping apples, even barn stored, will carry the handling and marketing season on until March or April.

As the land begins to dry, harrow and roller come out in grassed orchards, cultivator or disc harrow in arable, to turn in the weed growth or cover crop of autumn and winter. The buds begin to move and the spraying programme begins; the grass starts growing and the mowing machine comes out; whatever has been left undone in the winter must remain undone.

Blossom time is always an anxious season, though attempts to avoid frost damage are confined to orchards in known frost holes. Spraying with water from a sprinkler throughout a frost has been shown to be effective in protecting the trees, though they may be damaged by the weight of ice; it is not likely to be practicable unless combined with irrigation equipment. Fog-making machines, to blanket radiation from earth to sky, have also been developed, but orchard heaters burning crude oil, or smoky bonfires of straw bales, old motor tyres and sump oil, remain the usual defence.

Routine spraying goes on again after blossom and at least until the end of June, by which time the sprayer will have been round a minimum of six times — three times before and three times after blossom. The tractor alternates between spraying and mowing or cultivating on any but large farms. Cultivation usually ends in July or August and thereafter weeds or sown cover crop are left to grow until the following spring. Grass cutting is likewise stopped by drooping branches, but the mower comes out again after harvest for a final round — the twelfth or more of the season. In either case young orchards require some hand-work, hoeing, hand-pulling or cutting weeds round the trees. Most orchards end up with a bed of couch round the tree stems, but weeds, and particularly couch, must be controlled in the early years; couch unrestricted can kill out trees on Type IX, and rough growth against tree stems harbours mice.

All through the summer the trees' performance reflects soil, season and management. As in other branches of agriculture, the master's foot is the best dung. Odd jobs keep showing up as soon as looked for. Where scab, canker or mildew are troublesome a partial second pruning in May can be necessary, to cut out dead wood or infected shoots missed in the winter. However well the spray routine may go, some pests and diseases remain for which spraying is either impracticable or ineffective. Spectacular defoliation of a young tree is often the sign of enormous eyed hawk-moth caterpillars, which must be picked off by hand; an occasional wilting shoot or branch may be due to the drilling of a leopard moth caterpillar, leaving a telltale hole and a little heap of sawdust; riddling the hole with a piece of bent wire is the remedy. Many other minor pests not controlled by routine spraying may call for attention as soon as their characteristic damage is seen. Birds incidentally do not know their job; where caterpillar damage shows there is nearly always a live caterpillar to be found and not one conspicuous by its absence. Whether or not birds do any good by stealth early in the season their damage later on is only too obvious. Blackbirds are the worst. Most growers make some attempt to keep birds away by some form of visual or automatic noise-making scarer, but a man perpetually going round with a gun is really the only effective protection for more than a few days. Rooks are not apple-eaters, but they can be infuriating in a young orchard, scattering the mulch in search of food and breaking off shoots wholesale by their blundering flapping and perching. Apart from birds, the major apple-eating pests are wasps, which can only be destroyed nest by nest; it is worth offering a reward for nests found to boys on holiday. Earwigs or dock sawfly caterpillars can also damage the ripening fruit and may be controllable by spraying the tree stems and surrounding ground with an insecticide. Grease-banding is now hardly used in commercial orchards, and the old lime-washing of the tree trunks was never more than ornamental.

Thinning begins in July, and where a range of varieties is grown leads on into picking without a break. Some tying-up or propping of laden branches is often necessary, and the spraying machine comes out again if a pre-harvest hormone spray is being used to prevent premature drop of the fruit. Apple harvest at its fullest possible stretch lasts from early August with Beauty of Bath to mid-November with Wagener and Granny Smith; one pair of hands can pick a great many apples in that time, it is the necessary concentration of big blocks of few varieties that makes the rush. The autumn grass picks up after all the trampling, and the mower makes one more round. The last leaves fall and pruning can begin again – in really good time – just as soon as the crop is out of the way. The struggle to be 'up with the work' is on once more; how easy if apple trees did not have to bear apples.

The same jobs fill the seasons in old orchards and new, but only in new plantations can the routine be eased and possible new practices allowed for by thoughtful planning before planting, matched by foreseen management after-wards. More and more control can be expected to come from the spraying machine, not merely of pests and diseases but hormonal control of blossom and fruit, control of nitro-gen status and mineral deficiencies by foliage sprays, perhaps even control of pollination by sprays of pollen or of hormonal substitute. The necessity of suiting tree arrange-ment and form to the demands of automatic spraying is a novel idea at present, but everything points to its becoming commonplace : growing the tree for the inflexible machine instead of designing the machine for the awkward tree, as at present. This means, first, a rectangular plant – hedge-like rows of trees separated by wide alleys – and second, reasonably low trees trained to a delayed open centre form with a central stem, like oversized dwarf pyramids. Even if some routine spraying should eventually (but within the lifetime of an orchard planted now) be superseded by soil applications of systemic insecticides and fungicides, making the sap toxic, a rectangular plant still has the advantage in all other mechanical operations, whether spreading fertilizers and manures, carting fruit or cultivating and mowing; the advantage will be particularly marked if cutting grass in the alleys to mulch the tree-rows turns out to be better than close overall mowing.

Soil management and other practices are always changing, but once the trees are planted they are there for good, and once their framework is built up it is fixed. The only clear trend in fruit-growing, as in nearly every other activity, is towards more machines and fewer men; the only means whereby new orchards can match the machine is in tree arrangement and tree building; the rest must be left to the future.

APPENDIX

For orchards in bearing

Quantities given are to make 100 gall. of spray. Mature bush trees require 200–300 gall. per acre. Follow manufacturers' advice about addition of wetting agents, usually necessary in post-blossom sprays.

    (i) 4–6 gall. DNOC at bud break (mid-March) for eggs of aphis, sucker and red spider.

    (ii) 2–2½ gall. Lime Sulphur at green cluster for scab *plus*

        2½ lb. DDT (20 per cent wettable powder) for winter moth and tortrix caterpillars, and for capsid.

    (iii) 1½–2 gall. Lime Sulphur at pink bud for scab.

    (iv) ¾–1 gall. Lime Sulphur *or*

        4 lb. Colloidal or Dispersible Sulphur at 80 per cent petal-fall for scab and mildew.

    (v) 8 oz. Nicotine *or*

        2 lb. BHC (50 per cent wettable powder) 7–10 days later for apple sawfly *plus*

        Fungicide as in (iv) for scab and mildew.

    (vi) 2 lb. Lead Arsenate at fruitlet (mid-June) for codlin moth *plus*

        4 lb. Colloidal or Dispersible Sulphur for scab and mildew.

Alternatives and Extras

Add 2½ lb. DDT (20 per cent wettable) to the DNOC spray if apple blossom weevil appears.

If DNOC is dropped or missed, use DDT emulsion or BHC, or a combination, at bud-burst to mouse-ear; and be prepared for summer spraying with derris or CPCBS against red spider. This may be necessary anyway.

Add 2 lb. lead arsenate to the pink bud scab spray if caterpillar is bad.

Where scab is very bad the ideal is a fungicide spray every 10–14 days from the beginning of April until July, including blossom-time. Where full strength lime sulphur is too damaging, it can be used at half strength plus 2 lb. of elementary sulphur, both before and after blossom.

If mildew is no problem captan or mercury can be substituted for lime sulphur or sulphur, either post-blossom or throughout.

A second lead arsenate spray for codlin many be necessary in early July. Mercurated lead arsenate conveniently combines scab and codlin control.

Attend to manufacturers' warnings about varietal susceptibilities and the compatibility of mixed sprays with great care.

RENEWAL PRUNING GUIDE

For bearing trees of average vigour

Cut out altogether any diseased, crossing, rubbing, overcrowded and heavily shaded shoots or branches.

Leaders.—Shorten leaders from which further extension growth or new branches are required by about one-third. Leave others untouched. Select a few upward growing shoots well in towards the middle of the tree as replacement leaders, and cut back to keep them growing.

Laterals.—Leave about two-thirds of the one-year-old laterals untouched, to go on and form blossom buds; cut the rest hard back to 3 in. stubs to grow out into further new laterals. When strong blossom buds have formed along two- and three-year-old laterals cut most of them back to about five buds.

Spurs.—Thin out overcrowded spurs and spur systems.

More vigorous trees, cut less; under-vigorous, cut harder.

MANURING GUIDE

For dessert apples in grass; bush trees in bearing and of average vigour

Winter or early spring dressings per tree, scattered under and beyond the spread of the branches.

Annually

½–2 lb. of 15–20 per cent inorganic nitrogen (Nitro-chalk, Sulphate of Ammonia or Nitrate of Soda); or organic manure to give equivalent nitrogen.

¼–½ lb. of Sulphate of Potash; or none in case of magnesium deficiency.

Renew mulches as appropriate.

Every 3 years

½ lb. of Magnesium Sulphate (Agricultural Epsom Salts) as a precautionary dressing; ½ lb. or more annually in case of deficiency symptoms, plus foliage spraying at 20 lb/100 gall., with a wetting agent.

About 4 cwt. per acre of Super-phosphate or about 10 cwt. of Basic Slag, broadcast.

BIBLIOGRAPHICAL NOTE

THREE comprehensive manuals are essential reading for any one seriously thinking of growing apples commercially. They are *Modern Fruit Growing* by W. P. Seabrook, *Good Fruit Farming* by C. R. Thompson, and *Apples and Pears*, the Ministry of Agriculture's Bulletin No. 133. Seabrook, long known as the fruit grower's bible, has run through innumerable editions and shows signs of the struggle to keep up to date; it is the best on the factory aspects of apple growing. Thompson is best on practical management, and the Ministry's Bulletin, largely written by research workers, admirably mixes the results of many trials with best commercial practice.

The two standard reference books on pests and diseases are Dr A. M. Massee's *The Pests of Fruits and Hops* (new edn 1954) and Dr H. Wormald's companion volume *Diseases of Fruits and Hops* (last edn 1946). The best guide to nursery work is *Fruit Tree Raising* (Ministry of Agriculture's Bulletin No. 135). There is much useful information in *The Fruit-Grower Year Book*, published annually. The two trade papers, mentioned in the first chapter, are *The Grower* and *The Commercial Grower*, both weeklies.

Printed in the United States
133208LV00002B/30/P